Gardens of War

Robert Gardner was born in 1925 and graduated from Harvard University
in 1948, and after studying and teaching in Istanbul and Seattle, Washing-
ton, he returned to Harvard to do graduate work in anthropology. In 1955
he became the first director of the Film Study Center at the University's
Peabody Museum. Prior to organizing and directing the Harvard-Peabody
Expedition to New Guinea he assisted in making an anthropological film
of the Bushmen in Africa's Kalahari Desert, and he has just completed a
similar study on Ethiopian nomads. *Dead Birds,* his film about the Dani of
the West New Guinea highlands who are the subject of this book, has won
world-wide honors — among them the 1963 Robert Flaherty Award, and
the Florence, Melbourne and Trento film festival awards.

Karl G. Heider was born in 1935, studied at Williams College and graduated from Harvard University in 1956. He spent the next year in Asia as a
Sheldon Travelling Fellow, and thereafter studied anthropology at the
University of Vienna in Austria. Returning to Harvard as a graduate
student, he was awarded his doctorate in anthropology by the University
in 1966. Karl Heider observed the Dani in the Baliem Valley for twenty-
six months, the last twenty-one months of this time alone, after the departure of the other members of the Harvard-Peabody Expedition.

Gardens of War

Life and Death in the New Guinea Stone Age

Robert Gardner and Karl G. Heider

Introduction by Margaret Mead

PENGUIN BOOKS

Penguin Books Ltd, Harmondsworth, Middlesex, England
Penguin Books Australia Ltd, Ringwood, Victoria, Australia

First published in the U.S.A. by Random House 1968
Published in the United Kingdom by André Deutsch 1969
Published in Penguin Books 1974

Pictorial illustrations copyright © 1968 by the Film Study Center,
Peabody Museum, Harvard University, Cambridge, Massachusetts

Made and printed in Australia by Alexander Brothers, Mentone, Victoria

For Lee

Introduction by Margaret Mead

This is a book for those who enjoy looking, through the eyes of others and the mediation of the still camera, at scenes that they themselves are most unlikely ever to see. It is unique. Never before has such a diverse group, with such diverse interests and skills, on a complex and lengthy expedition into primitive territory, taken so many pictures that it became possible to select from among thousands a set of pictures which fit together so well that the identity of the individual photographer is almost obscured. Putting together a collaborative photographic book is one of the more felicitous forms of cooperative authorship, even when the photographs are all taken by the same photographer, or when a group of authors select from a given corpus, as was done in *The Family of Man*. For battles over words and phrases and ideas, one can substitute the expressive "But look, surely *this* one makes the point better than *that* one does." Alternative photographs can be arranged as the authors, guided by their central theme, work out their plans in a series of choices.

All of this has happened before. But in *Gardens of War* something even more complex has been attempted. The photographs by all the members of the expedition became the corpus from which this book was built. Its unity, and no one who enjoys the book will dispute this unity, is provided by the Dani themselves, by the coherence of their Stone Age culture, by the harmony existing between one aspect of their ancient warlike way of life and another, by the metaphor of singing birds and the life of the people.

The book's essays provide background information which could only have been obtained by anthropologists working carefully and soberly to explore the intricacies of the Dani culture. They serve as notes to some of the less easily comprehended pictures. But essentially this is a visual book, a record of what any Western reader might have seen, had he a trained eye, if he had been set down suddenly among the Dani. That such a reader could never experience this abrupt transition—except as a result of a plane accident that would leave him little time for marveling at the people around him—is beside the point. To take these pictures meant many months of patient work, establishing a base, learning to speak and to know and understand the people. But the photographs themselves are of what any one of us might have seen had we been able to go there. They are not candid camera shots stolen surreptitiously from an unaware people; they are not constructed and reenacted events designed for the camera alone, divorced from real life and real participation. They were taken by those who were there—and *known* to be there—in the midst of a flourishing society.

Even to someone like myself with many years of experience in other parts of New Guinea, these pictures—like the film *Dead Birds,* of which this book is an accompaniment and a reminder, and Peter Matthiessen's book, *Under the Mountain Wall*—gave me fresh delight, as scenes that I had only heard of came vividly to life. There is a great difference between hearing from the lips of people to whom warfare has been forbidden what war once was like; or in watching a warrior who no more will go to war stand and tighten his now-unused bow; or in straining one's imagination to recapture a scene now immortalized only in memory—and, on the other hand, having a visual record of how such warriors really confront each other across a traditional battlefield. I have often found the accounts of such warfare hard to credit because usually they are recounted in words that run something like this: "We met on the mountainside near Wihun. A man of our side, named Maigi, threw a spear at a man of their side, named Wea. He missed. Then a man of their side threw a spear and hit my cross-cousin from Ahaleseimihi. Then I was angry and threw a spear at Wena, a big man of their side, and missed..." and so on. Listening to such a verbal account, one cannot help wondering what everybody else was doing. How could an individual single out a sequence like this from a battle? The material on the Dani in this book illuminates such a question—and many others. We see the warriors of each side, magnificently attired, widely dispersed, few of them at any one moment heavily engaged, and thus responsive to the wounding of one man.

In one anthropological account after another I had read of the custom of sacrificing a finger joint when a relative died. No imagining can equal a picture of a woman with only stumps on her hands working or caring for a child. The word "sacrifice" suddenly assumes new meaning; man's capacity to contrive terrible and unnatural cruelties throws a new light not only on New Guinea, but on the battlefields of later wars, and on the mourning women who live on after the battles are over.

One of the most conspicuous things about the cultures of preliterate peoples like the Dani is that it is their whole way of life that is a creation—unique, evanescent, dependent for its very existence entirely on the continued practice of each generation. Such people, even those more artistic than the Dani, leave us only a handful of artifacts to remember them by. Unless we can record with film and tape the sights and sounds of their life, the world loses—and loses forever—part of the rich repertoire of the past on which we must depend to understand the future. That is what we have here: an array of pictures that will remain long after the Dani—pacified, freed (possibly only unhappily) from the long, relentless cycle of killing and being killed, trapped perhaps in some less congenial treadmill of modern technological society—have ceased to live and move as they do now. They will continue to marry and bear children who carry the same genes as the men and women pictured here, but the culture which they embodied will be gone forever. In fact it is already well on its way to oblivion, even as we can turn these pages and discover them standing in their age-old postures, bow strings taut and heads erect.

It is hard to convey to anyone who has not been to New Guinea just how fragile such a moment is. If the anthropologist goes too far beyond the areas where government has sent patrols, missions have established advance stations and word of the expectations of the Western world has already spread, he risks spending an incredible amount of time in trying to learn a language without the help of interpreters, and in guarding life and property against attack. Having informants who may be killed in one's own back garden is a shattering experience, which no anthropologist who depends upon mutual trust willingly undertakes. Yet if the full flavor of the native style of life which is so soon to be altered is to be caught, he must go in ahead of the mission, and if he is interested in warfare, headhunting or cannibalism, he must be ahead of full pacification by government. He must, in fact, catch a culture trembling on the edge of change, but hopefully not yet altered by the knowledge that change is on its way. The Harvard-Peabody New Guinea Expedition was able to do just this. The Netherlands Government authorities fully approved the expedition, and so the dilemma of conniving in any way with breaking the law was removed. But only a month after the major part of the filming was completed, and most of the expedition had left, the Kurelu region where the expedition worked was pacified.

The records of the Dani's ritual warfare also owe a great deal to the peculiar nature of the New Guinea highland landscape, because its high visibility for many miles made it easy and safe to watch their battles. With a telephoto lens it was possible to film battles in which the film makers were not only not asked to take part, but of which they were not apprised in advance. Thus, ethical issues were fairly met, and later generations are permanently the wiser.

The roster of anthropologists who have lost their lives gives a heroic cast to the work of those who return to publish their work. The death of Michael Rockefeller on his second expedition to New Guinea, and the week-long anguished search in which people all over the United States participated vicariously, brought anthropological work in general, and the Dani expedition in particular, close to Americans, who like to follow their own countrymen into faraway places. The fact that this particular book is a romantic one, owing much of its appeal to the huge distance between the Dani way of life and ours, adds to its appeal. *Gardens of War* is a valuable part of what we owe to this expedition to the Dani.

Margaret Mead
The American Museum of Natural History
New York

Foreword

More than seven years have passed since the day that members of the Harvard-Peabody New Guinea Expedition left the Dutch government post of Wamena and first set foot in the world of the Dugum Dani. The months following that first February morning in 1961 when Jan Broekhuijse, Abututi and I looked at the villages in which we would live were filled with an astonishing assortment of experiences that none of us from half a world away would have imagined possible.

Abututi is a Dani, and he and Jan were the first bridges between our own culture and that of the Dani. But even Jan, though never as bewildered as the rest of us, was often amazed by what he saw. He had been trained in anthropology and sociology at the University of Utrecht, and his great love was New Guinea. At that time he was serving as a district officer for the Netherlands Government, which until 1962 administered the western half of the immense island, now part of Indonesia and called West Irian. When the expedition was organized, the government detached Jan from his regular duties in a neighboring valley so that he could gain information about the people of the Grand Valley of the Baliem prior to our arrival. That he succeeded despite a variety of setbacks testifies both to his determination and to his remarkable devotion.

Almost a year before it finally set forth, the expedition had begun in Cambridge, Massachusetts. At Harvard University's Peabody Museum, the oldest institution in America for the study of people and their cultures, I had recently organized the Film Study Center for anthropological film research. There was, I felt, no doubt that even if the more ambitious aims of anthropology were only indirectly served and no startling discoveries were made about the still-mysterious "laws of human behavior," creating a careful and sensitive visual account of an unknown society was ample justification in itself.

Curiosity about one's fellow creatures is a hallmark of civilization. Should we ever lose interest in the way others live and look, we will have lost an important aspect of our humanity. This curiosity is not idle or sentimental; rather, it is a seeking to know about others' circumstances so as to better identify oneself and to see a little more clearly the direction in which we might wish our own identities to evolve. What might, then, seem no more than a colossal vanity may actually be the mainspring of our moral natures. By our very eagerness to find out about others and in our willingness to use this knowledge as a mirror, we can progress surely, if often slowly, down the road of human change and betterment.

Man's great distinction is surely not his erect posture, which has not changed in hundreds of thousands of years, but his self-consciousness, which has created an endless variety of lifeways. Indeed, change has so accelerated in the past few hundred years that it threatens to leave us poorer instead of richer. Surely one of the most tragic themes of this century is the inexorable and irreversible decline of traditional societies and their values throughout the world. The anthropologist in every man has fewer and fewer human alternatives to contemplate, fewer and fewer lessons to learn in the contrasts of other men's behavior and ideas. It must also be lamented that only a pitifully small sample of this incredibly diverse legacy of human inventiveness has been recorded—and virtually the entire record is verbal. Of course we are grateful for something like Bernardino de Sahagun's literate and absorbing account of sixteenth-century Aztec society; without it, our understanding of that remarkable civilization would be far less perfect than it is. But today, after five hundred years of advances in technology and awareness of what ought to be preserved of the human chronicle, we are in a position to give to the centuries that follow a far more complete and vivid picture of societies that in splendor rival the Aztec and, like the Aztec five hundred years ago, are now on the brink of extinction.

It is a curious irony that the societies that have brought on the ruin of technologically inferior cultures have also invented instruments for preserving extremely lifelike records of their victims. These instruments have been available since the beginning of this century, when men took history's first motion pictures of the world around them. These jerky and obscure vignettes of ordinary events, capturing in a faltering manner a few moments of time and space, are real treasures. If today we are excited by a film of workers leaving a French factory in 1910, it is because this magic medium has allowed us to reexperience an actuality that time has erased.

The popularity of movies throughout the world today proves that we have some concern for the record of our own life. But what of the rest of the world? By the year 2000 human society promises to vary little from continent to continent. Transportation and communication will link the remotest valley and farthest plateau with centers of technology. Deserts will be watered, marshes drained, and the cultures that developed in response to isolation or hardship will have disappeared.

Hence it was partly in the spirit of conservators of a passing age that we planned the Harvard-Peabody New Guinea Expedition. When the possibility of sending an expedition to do film and anthropologic research first arose, perhaps the most difficult task was to choose among several areas urgently requiring such study. In Africa, for example, there still survive a few nomadic herders, once widespread. It is only a matter of decades before such people as the Bororo, the Fulani or the Afar will abandon their wandering lives and settle near growing numbers of artificial wells drilled by governments that prefer settled to nomadic herdsmen. Michael Rockefeller, who when still a senior at Harvard was the most enthusiastic and generous stimulant to our venture, had particular curiosity about South America. Furthermore, on that continent there exist more diverse tribal societies, much of them unstudied and some of them still undiscovered, than perhaps anywhere else in the world.

It was my own hope to make a study of a society still practicing what in anthropological annals is known as "ritual warfare" that turned our attention to Melanesia. I had often wondered about the differences between ordinary and ritual warfare. As a child I spent long hours on the floor of my parents' library turning the pages of bound volumes of *The London Illustrated News,* especially those of the years 1914 to 1918. These photographs told me about the most exciting and terrible game anyone could possibly play. Two teams, one in khaki with hats like inverted soup plates, the other in gray with spiked coal scuttles on their heads, tried with all their might to go in opposite directions without getting killed. Then I learned about other people in other books, and that ever since time began, this game was always being played somewhere in the world.

Years later I wondered if there could possibly be people who thought war was other than a necessary evil, who practiced what anthropologists call ritual warfare. "Ritual" means that it is regularly repeated and indispensable. Common warfare is rationalized in a different way and is not sacred but profane. Most of all, I wondered if a greater understanding about violence in men could be achieved if it was studied in a metaphysical context completely different from our own. I wanted to see the violence of war through altogether different eyes, and I dared hope that new thinking might follow from such an altered perception. For this reason I was eager to go to New Guinea and into the Central Highlands, where men from villages separated only by their own gardens had been killing each other for as long as we have known that they lived there.

A unique opportunity presented itself. I was introduced to Dr. Victor J. DeBruyn, then director of the Bureau of Native Affairs in Netherlands New Guinea. DeBruyn knew western New Guinea well; he had studied it as an archaeologist and anthropologist, lived in its interior as an agent for Allied intelligence during World War II, and administered to its needs as a developing country. He wanted the Peabody Museum to do research there, and he felt confident that the program of pacification started ten years earlier by his government in the Highlands had by no means achieved complete success.

The expedition was a three-year undertaking that began with my own departure for New Guinea in February, 1961. For the preceding month Jan Broekhuijse was already in the field, though not in what was to be our ultimate locality. I knew only that we were going to the Grand Valley of the Baliem River, discovered by Richard Archbold during his botanical and zoological explorations in the New Guinea Highlands in 1938. It was this valley that received momentary notoriety in 1945 as a "Shangri La" when an American nurse, part of a group of sightseers on an excursion plane out of wartime Hollandia, survived a crash and was rescued with two male companions by an elaborate glider operation. The Grand Valley is about forty miles long by ten miles wide, and its Dani population is estimated to be as much as one hundred thousand. In 1961 the only nonindigenous people were either government workers manning the post at Wamena in the southern part of the Grand Valley, or missionaries who had opened stations and airstrips in various parts of the valley.

I had already had the benefit of DeBruyn's counsel about the extent of government influence in the valley. Evidently there were a few government patrols, consisting occasionally of a doctor, one or two native medical assistants and a handful of native police with their young Dutch patrol officers; these few attempted to bring health and peace to an area of hundreds of square miles and a population of extraordinarily independent people. But though parts of the Grand Valley had been pacified, there were still large areas subject to only nominal control. In searching for a Dani group as little changed by the outside world as possible, I learned that we would have the best luck in the Kurelu, a place named for the most powerful man living there. This district lay well to the northeast, somewhere close to the mountain wall, where it met the pass through which planes from Hollandia penetrated the ten-thousand-foot escarpment that encircles the Grand Valley.

There are missionaries in the Grand Valley and adjacent areas, Catholic and several denominations of Protestants, all in restrained competition with each other. The dominant group, in numbers and financial resources, is an organization called the Christian and Missionary Alliance. Its doctrinal roots are fundamentalist and its evangelical message reflects this. The people of the Kurelu had steadfastly refused to allow the bearers of this faith to settle in their area. In other Dani areas, their success in making "converts to Christ" seemed to be due more to a lavish use of trade goods and medicine than to propagation of a belief. Admittedly these observations are based on a limited series of experiences and impressions. There are many men of God in New Guinea who live and behave in harmony with their Christian precepts and who are a solace to any soul that comes within their ken. Others, though, constitute one of the profoundest risks confronting pagan man's entry into the contemporary world, a risk that those of the Kurelu had so far miraculously elected to avoid.

The Kurelu was about as untouched an area as an anthropologist is likely to find today. In the north, where Kurelu himself lived, a Dutch Franciscan missionary had established a post in December, 1960. Within twenty miles of our camp, there were approximately ten other missionary and government posts, some of which even had a short airstrip. But all this had surprisingly little influence on the lives of the Willihiman-Wallalua, the people of the southern Kurelu. For the most part the outsiders found work enough close at hand, and local rivalries and war frontiers discouraged the people of the southern Kurelu from visiting the missionary posts nearby. Missionaries had passed through the area, and a government patrol had even managed to establish a short-lived peace in 1959 or 1960. But by early 1961, when Jan and I first arrived, warfare had again begun and the only signs of outside influence were a few steel axes.

All of us except Karl Heider left the Dani in August, 1961. Within two weeks, the Dutch police had again pacified the area and built a patrol post a mile from our old camp. For the final twenty-one months of Karl's stay, the southern Kurelu was in a state of peace.

The organization of our expedition to the Baliem involved many unknowns. I had made a general plan for such an expedition even before it was certain that there would be one, but many unfinished details remained. DeBruyn had sent me rainfall and humidity charts made by the government post in Wamena, but for all their precision they told us little more than that the area was often wet. We knew nothing of the terrain except that it was difficult, nothing of transportation into the valley except that it was by small airplanes and often irregular because of rain or fog. We knew little about any hazards to health, of possible menace from the native population. We did know that beyond Wamena there were no roads, no vehicles and no beasts of burden. This meant that we must take the simplest possible equipment, and as little of it as we could. But even this was made difficult by our photographic and cinematographic objectives. Our plan was to choose a community of villages that would allow a group of as many as eight of us to stay for an indefinite period doing anthropological and photographic studies. Our number included Jan Broekhuijse as anthropologist and interpreter; Karl Heider as anthropologist and assistant cinematographer; Peter Matthiessen as naturalist; Michael Rockefeller as sound recordist and still photographer; and myself as cinematographer and part-time anthropologist. For shorter periods we were to be joined by Eliot Elisofon of *Life* and Samuel Putnam, then a medical student, also a photographer. Later Christopher Versteegh, a botanist who had been with Archbold in 1938, was to stay for two weeks, and Dr. Jan Pouwer, then a Netherlands Government anthropologist, also paid us a brief visit.

The overall aim of the expedition was to make a comprehensive study of a single community of neolithic warrior farmers. We intended to document verbally and visually the whole social and cultural fabric of this community. We were interested in its natural history and were equipped to scrutinize it from the standpoint of behavioral scientists, naturalists, photographers and film makers. Our specific goals included an ecologically oriented account by Peter Matthiessen (*Under the Mountain Wall,* published in the fall of 1962 by Viking); my feature-length motion picture (*Dead Birds,* released by Contemporary Films and Mutual Distributors for nontheatrical and theatrical showing in 1963); an anthropological monograph dealing with the whole culture (presented as his Ph.D. thesis at Harvard in 1965 by Karl Heider); a second anthropological monograph by Jan Broekhuijse (published as his Ph.D. dissertation at Utrecht in 1967); and a book of photographs.

The final goal is realized in this volume. It was finished later than intended because originally it was to have been written by someone else. When Michael Rockefeller came for a short visit to Cambridge in the fall of 1961, we looked over the photographs made up to that time. It was clear that Michael was pleased with what he saw, and he asked if he might assume the major responsibility for putting together the photographic book. I knew that he had virtually committed himself to returning to Harvard as a graduate student in anthropology, and since this meant that he would be in the proximity of the photographs for a period of at least three years, his offer seemed both timely and sensible.

But Michael never returned from his second journey to New Guinea. This book is not really mine. I would not have written it if Michael had lived, and it would never have been finished without the help of Karl Heider, whose twenty-six months in the Grand Valley mean that he knows far more than I about the Dani. My coauthor is junior only in respect to age. This book represents a true collaboration, though he was primarily responsible for the captions and I for the essays. Further, close friends and colleagues at the Carpenter Center for the Visual Arts at Harvard University have given this volume the benefit of their considerable gifts: Eric Martin in design; Len and Susan Gittleman in reproduction; and Erika Deutsch in patient translation from longhand to typeface.

Finally, this book belongs to all whose photographs speak so eloquently from its pages. There was a near din of clacking shutters every day and on many nights of our stay. We each had other duties, but no one could escape the photographic mania. For the others, as well as for myself, making pictures was one way in which we could attempt to honor the extraordinary richness of life confronting us. It was also, I think, a way for all of us to try to create the evidence which one day might be refined by the senses into more articulate answers to the endless questions crowding our minds as we underwent the eyewitness experiences of a lifetime. During those months one of Michael Rockefeller's most frequent expressions was "It's unbelievable." His photographs in this book and the photographs of my other companions say "It *is* unbelievable—and perhaps, by looking hard enough and long enough, you will understand it too."

Robert Gardner

Acknowledgments

The Harvard-Peabody New Guinea Expedition would not have been possible without the assistance of many people and institutions. We are especially grateful to the former Government of Netherlands New Guinea, to the United Nations Temporary Executive Authority, and to the Republic of Indonesia, under whose administrations these photographs were taken; to the missionaries of the Order of St. Francis, the Christian and Missionary Alliance, and the Missionary Aviation Fellowship; to the staff of the Peabody Museum of Harvard University and particularly its director, Professor J.O. Brew; to Leonard Brass, who accompanied Archbold on his 1938 expedition; to Dr. Harold J. Coolidge, who has long served the interest of science and exploration around the world; and to Dr. Victor J. De Bruyn, to whom he introduced us and whose help was always indispensable; and for funds, to the Peabody Museum, the Government of Netherlands New Guinea, the National Science Foundation, the Norman Fund, the National Geographic Society and private sources.

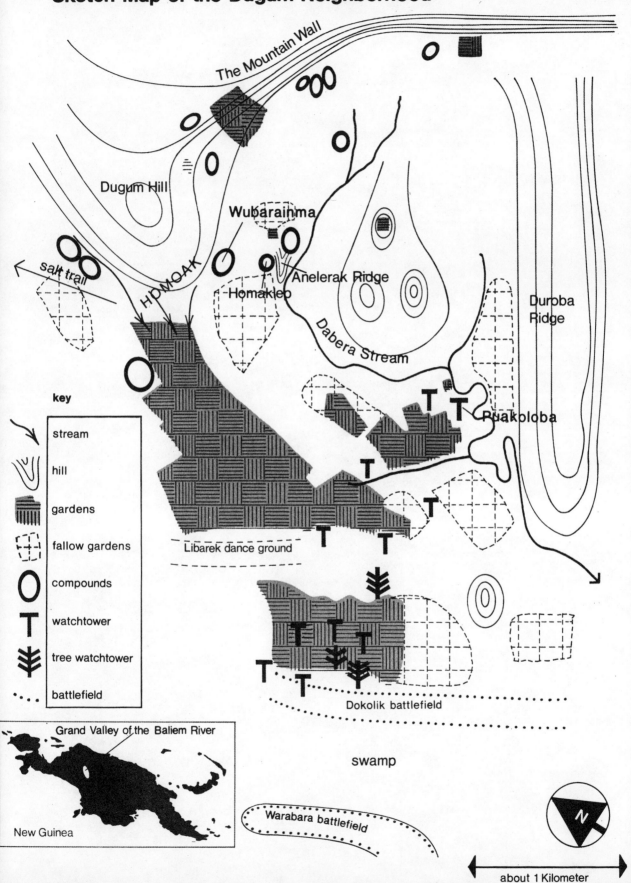

Sketch Map of the Dugum Neighborhood

The Mountain Wall

Dugum Hill

Wubarainma

salt trail

HOMOAK

Anelerak Ridge

Homakleo

Dabera Stream

Duroba Ridge

Puakoloba

key

- stream
- hill
- gardens
- fallow gardens
- compounds
- watchtower
- tree watchtower
- battlefield

Libarek dance ground

Dokolik battlefield

swamp

Grand Valley of the Baliem River

New Guinea

Warabara battlefield

N

about 1 Kilometer

Contents

Gardens of War

1 Appearances

There is a fable told by a mountain people living in the ancient highlands of New Guinea about a race between a snake and a bird. It tells of a contest which decided whether men would be like birds and die, or be like snakes which shed their skins and have eternal life. The bird won, and from that time all men, like birds, must die.
— from the film *Dead Birds*

Súe warek means "dead birds" in Dani, the language of tens of thousands of warrior farmers living in a contemporary Stone Age society high in the central mountain fastness of West New Guinea. Among these people a man's weapons and ornaments lost in battle are called Dead Birds. So also are any other parts of him such as his hair, which, should he lose his life, would be captured as well. The story in which the Dani recount the race between a bird and a snake is their mythological justification of the fact of death. Further, it is also the inspiration for an illusion that to be alive is also, in some important ways, to be a bird.

Early in March, 1961, Jan Broekhuijse and I awoke at the top of a limestone ridge that pointed eastward from the base of a low and lonely hill in the middle of a flat and fertile valley named for the great wandering Baliem River. We had come upriver in an outboard motor boat loaned to us by the head of the Dutch government station a few miles downstream. With us was Abututi, our interpreter, temporarily detached from his duties as a native policeman. Our plan was to explore the valley from its midpoint in the hope of finding a community of Dani villages that lay beyond the sphere of government or missionary influence. The region we sought was reputedly controlled by a man named Kurelu, which means "wise

egret," but refers as much to his singular lightness of skin as to his renowned craftiness.

As a district officer, Jan had visited many parts of the valley and once had even encountered Kurelu. The meeting took place to the north of the area we studied through binoculars on this first morning of our search and at the end of a long and tiring patrol. In the decade of their infrequent relations with the outside world, the Dani had acquired a reputation for hostile and even treacherous behavior, particularly in their contacts with missionaries and government officials. On his first meeting, Jan was too exhausted to test the strength of his authority in the face of Kurelu's obvious displeasure at finding a *waro* or reptile, as whites are known in Dani, patrolling his territory. Though Jan knew that Dani belligerence was much inflated in the stories told by panic-stricken missionaries, several of whom had been roughly handled but none ever killed in the Baliem, he also knew that a certain kind of violence was a rule and not an exception in the Dani way of life. So, with an exchange of greetings, probably the traditional *Eyak nyak halabok* (Hey, friend, I eat your feces), they parted, neither expecting nor hoping to meet again.

For some time we sat gazing out across the valley floor, slowly accustoming our eyes to the terrain. Near its eastern limit a series of slopes and hills carried upward a succession of gardens, forests and villages wrapped in groves of banana trees. It was impossible to see people at such a distance, but columns of smoke rising in the still morning air showed they were awake and preparing a meal. Closer by, in all directions below our limestone lookout, were similar concentrations of houses shaded by a few trees and surrounded by a mosaic of gardens separated by the functional geometry of their irrigation canals. However, my eyes kept returning to the villages under the mountain wall. Those on the nearby valley floor looked hot and dull, whereas on the opposite slopes and hills I could see forests and the dark lines of shaded brooks, all contributing to a far more congenial landscape.

At the base of one particularly prominent foothill that appeared to be a major buttress of the escarpment wall behind, grew a deep green grove of araucarias. These were the tallest trees left standing in the valley. Though not as beautiful as the graceful casuarinas forming arabesques along the banks of the Baliem, nor as delicately pretty as the feathery acacias that still clung to the sides of certain smaller streams, the araucarias had a monumental and primitive stateliness. Perfectly straight, they grew well over one hundred feet high with equally straight limbs at right angles along their entire length. The araucaria has the archaic look so frequent in the flora and fauna of New Guinea. Its convoluted bark and packets of spiny seeds seem natural in a land of tree kangaroos, grass-eating rats as large as sheep, great leathery-winged foxes and nonflying cassowary birds. Only the flying foxes lived on in the valley—many, apparently, in the araucaria forest.

How peaceful the valley looked that first morning. It was impossible to believe the terrified reports I had read at the New York headquarters of the Christian and Missionary Alliance a few months earlier. Even in talks with the missionaries I met at the government station in the valley, I had gained the unmistakable impression that the Dani were deceitful and barbaric pagans driven by the devil to loot and kill as they fancied. The evidence so far indicated something altogether different. Impeccable gardens covered the slopes coming down to the Baliem, and all along its banks freshly hewn planks stood in neat

bundles waiting to be carried to a village under construction. From what I could see, the valley was a vast and fertile farm where diligence played an unusually important role, because people, rather than animals, did all the work. It did not seem an easy life as much as a good one. The unhurried but purposeful activities of these ingenious farmers generated a distinctly rural and tranquil atmosphere.

For this reason it was doubly shocking to see, a mile or so in front of the villages we were exploring through binoculars, indisputable evidence of hostility—watchtowers of lashed poles standing about four hundred yards apart along an irregular frontier as far as the eye could see. Clearly the people we were watching were not only farmers, but warriors. I remembered a photograph in the files of the American Museum of Natural History made by the people who, in 1938, discovered the Baliem. It was taken as their sea plane swooped low over some gardens to land on the only straight section of the river near the place where the government station now stands. The photograph showed a Dani in a watchtower and his companions below it shooting arrows at the noisy invader which had violated their frontier and which, for the defenders, must have shaken their long-standing faith in their first line of defense. Now planes fly fairly regularly, carrying officials and missionaries up and down and in and out of the valley. They are called *ané wu,* which simply means "the voice of wu," the Dani approximation of reciprocating engines. The tribe is amused by them and no longer wastes arrows trying to kill them.

We decided to go to the villages beyond the watchtowers. Jan, Abututi and I had come with few belongings, both because we wanted to move easily and because we planned to return to the government station within a week or ten days. This journey was for the purpose of finding a place in which, with our companions from America, we could spend a long time. But though we had brought little baggage, there was more than the three of us could carry, and so we went for help to a nearby village. For the rest of the morning we tried to persuade some young men to go with us across the valley. They were extremely reluctant despite our assurances that no harm would come to them, for they were enemies of the people we wished to visit under the mountain wall, and they felt that if they went there they would be killed. We assured them that one of us would escort them back the next day and that during the night we would protect them, but our arguments seemed futile. What I did not know until much later was that their own argument was equally rational, and it was not until we had talked for a long time and offered an irresistible number of cowrie shells that three of them finally agreed to join us.

There was no Dani community, no matter how remote or independent, which by 1961 had not heard about the white people who had come to live in their valley. It was also true that experience had taught the Dani to fear as well as deplore these white men. The Dani we met across the valley would be afraid of us—afraid that we had come to steal their pigs, to take their women, perhaps to set fire to their holy objects with promises of salvation and a better life, and certainly to warn them against further warfare with their neighbors.

Still, we felt confident about our meeting. First, we were completely independent; we were neither missionaries nor agents of the government. We had no message, either spiritual or mundane, to impart, and no advice to give or demands to make. In fact, we wished to disturb the lives of the Dani as little as possible. Secondly, we were accompanied by Abututi, a Dani himself, whose belief in our sincerity and whose total familiarity with the behavior and values of those with whom we hoped to live meant that our chances of explaining the purpose of our visit were extremely good. Thirdly, I had carried all the way from the cabinet of a shell collector in Newton Upper Falls, Massachusetts, a perfect specimen of Cymbium diadema, an object prized above almost all others by the Dani, who cut them into irregular saucers to wear as necklaces and exchange for pigs or other wealth. Everything I had read or been told about the Baliem Valley included detailed and indignant accounts of Dani avarice, from which I concluded that they respected wealth and responded to the influence of economic power. Indeed, I suspected that achievement in their society was to a large extent measured by one's ability to command and manipulate commodities of all kinds, including food, ornaments, pigs and even women. I was not quite ready to regard the Dani as a grasping barbarian who with unabashed greed spends his days making petulant and sometimes violent demands upon any stray visitor. What I was to learn later was that despite the frequency of Dani demands, their manner was seldom fierce and often full of a kind of comic grace. It also seemed likely that with their clarity of mind the Dani recognized in the warmly clothed, well-fed and comfortable white man a logical benefactor to whom he could turn for amelioration of his own lot. In any case, Jan and I were hopeful that the great shell would serve its purpose.

It was midday when our small party set out across the valley. The morning haze had burned away and only a few high clouds crowned the peaks along the mountain wall. The sun shone brightly in the valley, more than a mile high, whose river, the Baliem, begins at ten thousand feet amid a multitude of nameless streams that drain the midsection of a great watershed running the whole length of New Guinea. From this height the Baliem falls in a torrent to the floor of the Grand Valley and meanders in the fashion of a true river to a gorge forty-five miles to the southeast. There it descends abruptly five thousand feet to the lowlands, where, changing color and pace, it carries the mud of the notorious southern swamps languidly out to the Arafura Sea.

Our reluctant helpers led us down a dry path past dead fires and off the limestone hill where we had slept. The Dani called this hill the Siobara, and though too rocky to garden, it clearly had its uses. The fires, we were told, had been lit for warmth while men waited for the sun and watched their enemies across the valley to the east.

On the valley floor it was much harder to see our destination, partly because of the change in perspective and partly because one's whole attention was required merely to walk. As I tested my balance scuttling across mud-greasy poles spanning each garden ditch, it occurred to me that our promise of safe conduct to our three reluctant porters must seem more ridiculous with every step. Surely they must have wondered how two men with their eyes fixed on the ground and their arms waving to maintain equilibrium could ever detect, much less defend against, a sudden and concealed attack.

Confidence, an indispensable attitude when one is faced with negotiating Dani footpaths, grew with each awkward step as we made our slow and alien way across the dull terrain separating the homeland of our helpers from the villages which were our objective. Later, after living among the Dani for some time, I learned that our hosts-to-be were following our progress that day with great interest. They had seen us, as a matter of fact, the evening before, as we made our camp on the Siobara. This was easy for them because their eyes are constantly searching the countryside for movement, especially in the territory of their enemy, and nothing is more conspicuous in this landscape than the shape, color and locomotion of fully clothed white men.

The terrain through which we walked that hot and expectant afternoon was composed of abandoned gardens, swamp and an occasional swale of short bushlike trees called *pabi,* meaning both excrement and enemy. It was a desolate no man's land—a land through which indeed no one would go unless to do violence to those beyond. Except for noise made by our feet and legs moving clumsily through a bog surrounded by high grass growing on former garden mounds, there was no other sound until, very suddenly, several men began running on both sides of us through the grass toward a spur of higher ground ahead. Apparently they had been escorting us for some time; now they declared themselves, since we had shown that their neighborhood must be our destination. Once on higher ground and past the screen of grass along the bog's edge, we found a group of perhaps fifty men—some standing, others seated on the ground, all watching as we approached. We were in a clearing about the size of a football field which I later learned was called the Libarek and was used for victory dances performed each time an enemy—man, woman or child—living on the other side of no man's land was killed.

Displaying as much assurance as we could muster, we approached a knot of three or four older men sitting a little apart from the others. My only thought was that if someone would listen to us, our purpose would be understood. After a prolonged period of greeting, during which time we also sat down, lit cigarettes and assumed as casual an air as circumstances allowed, we addressed ourselves to an alert, lean and prepossessing man of middle age who gave his name as Wali. Abututi explained to Wali that I had come from a place many days' walk away because I had heard that the people of this valley were such fine farmers and great warriors, and because I wanted to watch the way they lived. It was explained that we had gone to other places in this valley looking at many villages and gardens, but had not seen any as fine as those in this neighborhood with its hills, forests and streams under the mountain wall. I then asked Abututi to tell Wali that I and some friends who were coming to join me wanted to "sit down" with the people here for a long time. I added that I realized my request was large and that I did not want Wali or anyone else to think we were poor beggars without houses or gardens of our own. My wealth, I said, included many large shells which I would exchange for the privilege of living here.

To all of this Wali's quick mind responded with both dignity and decision. He wanted us to stay, and his friends would help by providing food and even houses for us to live in. He then mentioned that he would like to see one of my shells. The Cymbium diadema was carefully wrapped in one of the small boxes we had carried that afternoon from the Siobara. With Wali watching intently, I opened the box, but the shell had been only partly revealed when he pushed the wrapping back over it and asked that it be closed immediately. For a dreadful moment I wondered if my strategem in procuring the shell

had been in vain, but then I realized by the unmistakable look of cupidity in Wali's face that he wanted no one else to see what he already considered his.

Immediately Wali rose and told us to follow him to a place where we could sleep that night. By now it was twilight, the sun having set below the rim of the western wall. The air was cool and filled with the sound of warbling swallows making their daily midair feast on sleepy insects. Our three helpers from the enemy huddled in fear near Abututi, assuming that his policeman's rifle—which in fact was never loaded—would protect them from a growing circle of men and boys looking at us all with a mixture of bewilderment, curiosity and contempt. Wali had decided our fate. It was a brilliant and self-serving decision, fraught with potential good and evil. Would we make all of them rich, or only some of them? Would we take their women? Would we stop their wars?

Darkness came as though a curtain had been drawn, and as Wali's minions interrogated Abututi about Jan and me, our three porters faded into the night and returned to their villages. So fearful were they of losing their lives to the warriors of our new neighborhood that they did not even wait to receive their payment of cowrie shells.

1 Appearances

The faces of the Dani are like those of the other peoples who live in the thousand-mile-long mountainous heartland of New Guinea. These peoples, numbering hundreds of thousands, are called Papuans. The Papuans are not closely related in language, culture or race to the other peoples of the Pacific, the Malayo-Polynesians. Although anthropological research on the Papuans is far from complete, it now begins to appear that the different Papuan groups are racially, culturally and linguistically related to each other.

The land of these Dani is the Grand Valley of the Baliem River, a broad, temperate plain lying five thousand feet above the tropical jungles of New Guinea. At least fifty thousand Dani live in the densely settled valley floor, and another fifty thousand inhabit scattered settlements along the steep-sided valleys around the Grand Valley. Temperature is mild, rainfall moderate, wildlife harmless and disease rare; this is surely one of the most pleasant corners of man's world.

p. 11 : **1.** A watchtower sentry looks out over no man's land on guard against a raiding party from the enemy side. Behind him, the people of his own alliance work and play in security.

p. 12 : **2.** A woman carrying her daughter crosses sure-footedly over a log bridge which spans a major irrigation ditch.

p. 13 : **3.** A man drinks from the Aikhé River.

p. 14 : **4.** Hugging themselves in the early morning cold, a man and three boys cross a ditch in a fallow garden.

p. 14 : **5.** Amused by some joke, a man carries his stone ax on a shoulder scarred by an old arrow wound.

p. 15 : **6.** Sitting beside the hearth of his village men's house, Weyak smokes a cigarette of Dani tobacco through a long reed holder. In the rafters and on the walls are carefully wrapped bundles of magical goods and ornaments belonging to men who share this house.

pp. 16–17 : **7.** Two young boys whisper their secrets.

p. 18 : **8.** Downstream, in the heart of the enemy Wittaia's country, elaborate bridges are thrown across the Aikhé to connect villages and gardens.

p. 19 : **9.** A young man, ornamented for battle, has rubbed soot and pig grease on his hair, body and cheekbones.

p. 19 : **10.** Until they are four or five, little girls often have trouble staying well dressed.

p. 19 : **11.** A woman on her way to a garden wears a net down her back and carries her all-purpose digging stick. She hugs herself in the cold, showing the stumps on her left hand where, as a child, she lost her fingers at a funeral.

p. 19 : **12.** A young girl in a very dilapidated skirt, her body smeared with clay, hugs herself in the typical Dani reaction to cold.

p. 19 : **13.** At battle, men decorate themselves with pig tusks in their noses, furred and feathered headdresses and chest ornaments of various shells.

p. 19 : **14.** A man looks warily about in the dark.

p. 19 : **15.** An old woman has smeared herself with mud both for decoration and for protection against the sun.

p. 19 : **16.** Recounting an old battle, a man makes the gesture of shooting an arrow.

p. 19 : **17.** The Dani have dogs, which are kept by those few men who occasionally hunt birds and furry marsupials in the forests.

p. 19 : **18.** Feathers of many different birds, along with snail, cowrie and bailer shells, are the indispensable elements of Dani ornamentation.

p. 19 : **19.** A man counts "three" on his fingers.

p. 19 : **20.** The blossom of the sweet potato, the staple of Dani life.

p. 19 : **21.** Hubugaiyo is called **kepu** by the Dani, for he is at the bottom of Dani society. Perhaps he is mentally defective. Although he is not an outcast, he is a permanent bachelor, contributing little to the society and living on its very fringe.

p. 19 : **22.** Kurelu is the leader of the Loro-Mabel confederation, and the most important man of the entire alliance. He alone can initiate the great pig feast which occurs throughout the alliance approximately every five years.

p. 19 : **23.** A woman who lost four fingers as a girl smokes a cigarette.

p. 19 : **24.** A young girl.

p. 19 : **25.** A young man, ornamented for battle, plays a bamboo mouth harp.

p. 19 : **26.** A girl, her face smeared with mud, takes care of a younger village child while the mother is away.

p. 19 : **27.** There are few reptiles in the Grand Valley, and none of them are dangerous.

p. 19 : **28.** Although children may be old enough to eat regularly, they occasionally seek comfort at their mother's breast.

p. 20 : **29.** Pua, obliviously muddy from playing in the gardens.

p. 21 : **30.** In the early morning, pigs churn up mud in the courtyard of a Dani compound as the smoke from cooking fires seeps through thatch to mingle with low-lying clouds.

p. 21 : **31.** Boys frequently design play villages with araucaria seeds showing round men's and women's houses, long family houses and pigsties with their individual stalls.

p. 21 : **32.** From the air the four compounds of Wubarainma, together with the anthropologist's houses, appear to be a single village. Each compound is in fact a separate social unit, with its houses strung like beads on a single fence that encloses a common courtyard.

p. 22 : **33.** Late in the day a warrior, his bow and arrows over his shoulder, watches the closing moments of a battle.

[9]

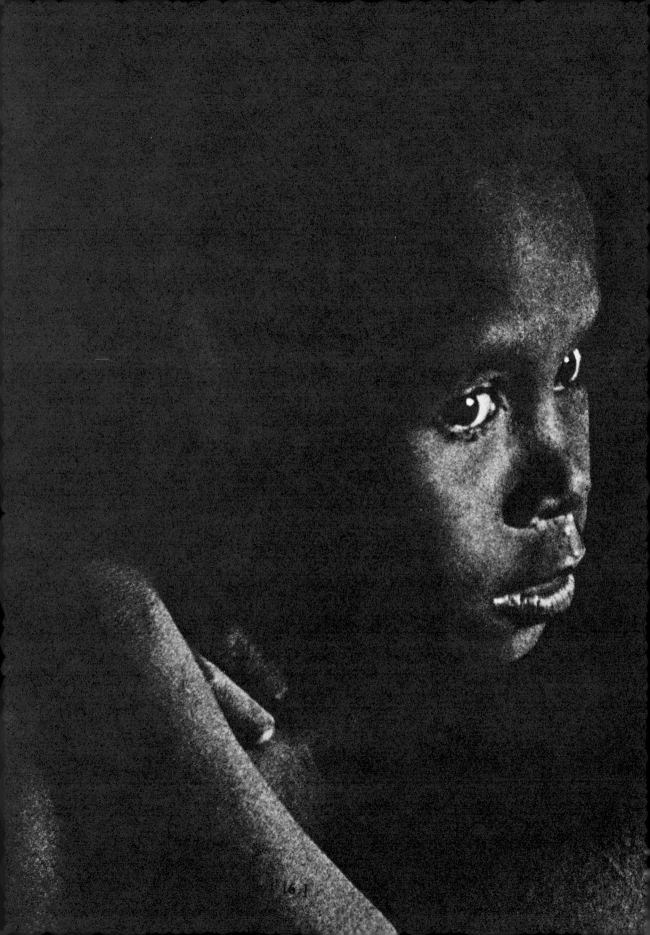

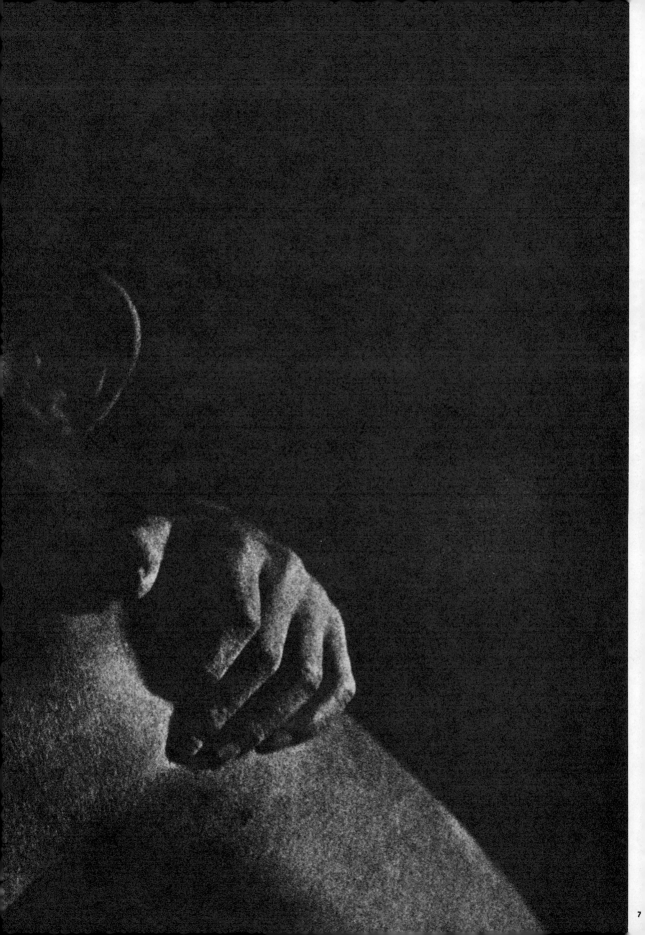

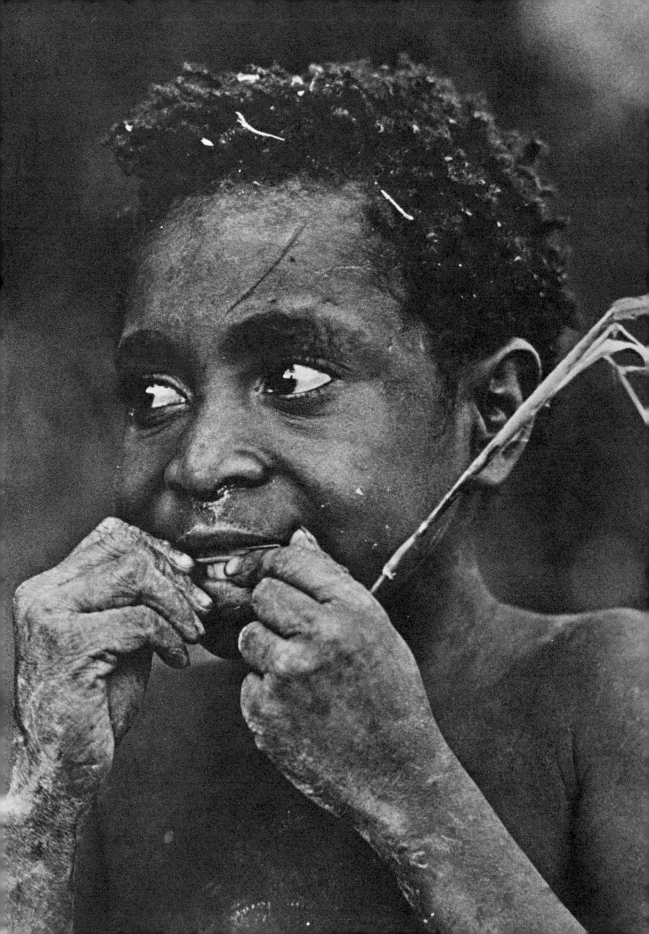

30

31

32

2 Skills

All expeditions are to some extent invasions. As a rule their goal is a place where they are not welcome, and most often they bring people and objects which are alien to the environment they invade. Despite our most sincere efforts, our arrival in a remote corner of the Baliem Valley was no exception. The contrast between ourselves and our belongings and the Dani and theirs was immense. They were dark brown and nearly naked; we were pink and overclad. We spoke different languages, walked with a different gait, ate different foods, even urinated in a different posture. Most of the people living near us had never been in close proximity to white men or their possessions. Within a matter of hours, however, for all but the shyest members of both worlds, our confrontation became an endless feast of mutual curiosity.

In the first weeks of our stay it was impossible to know what most interested the Dani about us, for there existed not only the barrier of language, but also that of continual perplexity and natural restraint. Often, especially among the men, I could detect a somewhat studied effort to be unconcerned. Sometimes a particularly important man would appear almost blasé. This was undoubtedly one of their ways of camouflaging their feelings of astonishment, envy and even resentment. The children were much freer of such tensions. Boys from about five to fifteen became our constant companions. They participated with all their senses in everything we did, and it was their almost immediate acceptance of us and our possessions which forged the first link between our worlds. For hours they would gape at such commonplace occurrences as the striking of a match or one of us brushing his teeth. But they were fair, and when we began to ask questions they provided answers and led us into their world.

For many days we simply absorbed the astonishing actualities of our new environment. In the forest of araucarias there was shade, a spring of cool fresh water, and sufficient cover to conceal our camp so that it did not mar the landscape. We made our permanent camp about a month after Jan and I had first walked across the valley, drawn by the same stand of dark woods into which we later moved. In the beginning we numbered five: Jan, Michael Rockefeller, Karl Heider, Peter Matthiessen and myself. Michael's assignments were sound recording, for which he had been trained in Cambridge, and still photography, for which he had a natural talent. Karl was the ethnographer, and his work with us (and on his own for another year and a half) was to result in his dissertation at Harvard. Peter had come to write a readable account of the whole natural fabric of Dani life, a task which he quickly and skillfully accomplished. My task was to coordinate all our activities and to pursue my major task of film making.

The Dani called our forest Homoak. It lay at the intersection of the valley floor and a foothill which sloped steeply upward toward the eastern wall. Around us were scattered several Dani settlements, the nearest a three-minute walk from our tents. Since this was also the village in which Wali spent much of his time, it was there that we went most often in the beginning. To say "village" is to use an expression which is only the nearest English equivalent to the Dani reality. Their settlements were really collections of compounds enclosed by a common fence or stockade. The fences were only to keep pigs from straying; they were too low and too insubstantial for fortification. Within the surrounding fence were four kinds of structures arranged according to a traditional though not inflexible pattern. At one end of the oval courtyard was the dominant dwelling—the circular domed men's house. On both sides were long rectangular family or cooking houses and smaller circular structures in which each woman slept with certain smáller children and her husband when he was not in the men's house. Finally there were houses divided into stalls where the pigs were kept.

A cluster of such compounds, in each of which perhaps two to five families might live, formed what I have called a village and what the Dani call a *sili*. Though the men of one *sili* are often related and there is usually a good reason, such as friendship or convenience to certain gardens, why individuals are in one *sili* rather than another, there is little feeling among the Dani of belonging or remaining in the *sili* of one's birth, childhood or marriage. They move frequently and unsentimentally from compound to compound, at least within the limits of a larger neighborhood.

On the third morning following our arrival we awoke to the sound of distant voices singing a high-pitched chorus far out on the dance ground to which Jan and I had come several weeks before. The noise sounded like some of the long and complex cheers one sometimes hears coming from a distant stadium on a clear autumn afternoon. Soon groups of men and women were congregating at various surrounding points: on hills, in little unplanted fields near some of the gardens and at lookout towers along the frontier beyond the furthest gardens. Eventually we learned that the voices we heard were raised in victory celebration. The songs were chants they would sing all day as they rejoiced at the news that an enemy had died from wounds received in a recent battle.

I was filled with an immediate sense of both satisfaction and concern; evidently our coming to Homoak had had no apparent effect on the behavior of those around us. It was ironic that this reassurance had first been obtained at the expense of the life of an unknown warrior, and I think all of us quickly understood the ethical dilemma of our situation.

The object of our visit was to study a living neolithic community, one of whose most distinctive traits was the practice of ritual warfare. We were privileged by education and equipment to document in writing, photographs, motion pictures and sound recordings everything that we could see or hear. This is no problem for efficient and properly functioning equipment: the lens sees and the microphone hears whatever they are shown. The difficulty lay in defining the degree to which we, as avowed observers, would permit ourselves to participate as people capable not only of expressing ideas or feelings, but also of exerting certain kinds of influence. Would we merely watch as a man beat his wife senseless for permitting herself to be "raped" by another man? Would we attempt to discourage a raid on an enemy garden? Would we refuse to provide medical assistance because we did not want to disturb the normal pattern, or because we felt it would give unfair advantage to the neighborhood in which we happened to be staying?

As it turned out, circumstances never afforded precise formulation of such moral problems. Wife beating was a private affair, and though I heard it happening several times, I saw it only once, from the top of a hill overlooking a village compound a quarter of a mile away. Raids and ambushes were even more secret, and we were never privy to the conversations which set them in motion. If we had tried to interfere once we knew they were in progress, we would have done so at some peril to ourselves—but far more to those involved. As for medical treatment, none of us had a medical degree and so we undertook as little amateur doctoring as possible. Only once did I take a real medical risk. It happened early in our stay, about a week following the first victory celebration. For several days a man from a distant but allied village asked me to see his son who was, he said, very sick. I put him off with a variety of excuses, saying that my medicine was not particularly strong or that I could not take the time to walk so far. Finally he persuaded me to see the boy. I found him very ill from an infected arrow wound in his back. I was told that part of the arrow had broken off and that they had been unsuccessful in their attempts to remove it all. I decided not to try to improve on their own surgery and gave the boy some penicillin, hoping the remaining splinters would be absorbed if the infection healed. Something of the sort apparently happened, for a few weeks later the boy came to give me his shy thanks.

Although at the time our first weeks seemed to be filled with extraordinary happenings, we soon realized that Dani life is characteristically vigorous, crowded with heavy work and punctuated with great events. Within the span of a few weeks we had witnessed a victory celebration, a pitched battle and a warrior's funeral. Connecting these vivid and momentous days was the thread of everyday life in a community that subsisted almost exclusively on the fruit of its own labors.

The Dani are inveterate and careful workmen. This observation was strengthened by the realization that we depended heavily on things made *for* us instead of *by* us. This was clear from the moment of our arrival. Our houses came out of duffle bags, our cigarettes out of packages, and much of our food out of tins. We could erect, but the Dani could build, and they did so avidly. Yet it seemed curious that though they gave arduous and conscientious effort to their tasks,

they seemed quite unpossessive toward and detached from what they had made. Eventually we discovered that other rules governed their attitudes about ownership, and that the relation between a person and his possessions was anything but casual.

Without appearing to enjoy the various tasks to which their hands constantly turned, the Dani nevertheless seemed reluctant to spend time in idleness. The degree to which one actually labored—except for women, who worked incessantly—depended on such factors as age and prominence. An old man with more than one wife and substantial wealth in pigs or shells did little or no heavy work. On the other hand, a young man not yet married had obligations that might keep him busy building a house or clearing garden land for many days at a time. Boys and girls from about the age of ten usually herded their family pigs. Since this was done in the morning, their tasks still left them half or more of every day to play. Often the children managed to play while watching their pigs, though this sometimes led to an animal's being lost or stolen and then to the guilty child's violent abuse by the owner. Younger children, including infants, stayed close to their mothers, whose principal labor outside the village was in the gardens.

Among the Dani, men are the creators and women are the producers. Men conceive and originate; women listen and follow. By Western standards there is vast inequality between the sexes, especially after childhood. Though industry was evident in both the male and female worlds, men preempted all the drama and excitement, while women were limited to a routine of drudgery. Such a difference in the very quality of experience had, it seemed, a depressive effect on most women. Many of them looked bored and sullen, whereas the men were characteristically gay and talkative. However, there was a distinctly nervous or at least cerebral quality to this gaiety, as if the men realized that the good fortune of being male might not last forever. Though I never asked them, it is probable that most Dani men would say they deserved their varied, if unquiet lives because of the risks they took in protecting their women and children, whether as sentries in the lookout towers or as warriors on the battlefield. However, it was apparent that these battles were fought as much to defend their masculine privileges as their families.

It would be a mistake to assume that no useful or routine work is done by Dani men. There is virtually no idleness among them, and they are constantly engaged in a variety of tasks. Their hands combine the attributes of strength and dexterity necessary for the difficult work of making a new garden, of dredging an old irrigation canal, of weaving a bracelet from fern fibers or of knitting long ceremonial bands from bark string. There is a distinctly Oriental facility and concentration in their handcrafting. Large and powerful men with well-deserved reputations as warriors and killers would sit for hours rolling beaten bark into string on their thighs, making skirts from orchid fibers for their wives, or plucking hair from a companion's chin with tweezers made from a half-broken twig.

Except for the time spent on their weapons— either fashioning new arrows and spears or decorating old ones with new string handles and white pigment—the men's occasional work was devoted largely to decorative rather than functional ends. Immense thought and effort were spent on attaining at least the minimal standards of male beauty. For the Dani such beauty does not depend on lavish or theatrical display. Though certain feathers, particularly those of the rare birds of paradise which now must be secured through trade with people in less populous valleys to the east, and certain shells, such as the

simple cowrie, a small sea snail and the great Bailer or Cymbium diadema, are much prized, such decorative wealth is worn only infrequently. Most often it was the men with the smallest feathers and fewest shells who wore them. In fact, for some weeks we were misled in our estimation of certain men's importance by assuming that their simple appearance meant that they were poor and lacked influence. The most influential war leader and one of the wealthiest men in the entire valley seldom wore any shells; even on the battleground, where almost every man decorated his head with feathers, he was unadorned except for a grass bracelet, some strips of matted spiderweb around his neck and the inevitable gourd to cover his penis.

The men's heavy work was eminently practical. They were the house carpenters, garden makers, ditch diggers, wood cutters and watchtower builders. Such labors seemed to proceed in individual spurts. Typically a man might spend an arduous week clearing a ditch in a garden from which he and those who helped him would later harvest a crop. Then for a week or more he might do no heavier task than gathering leaves in the hills above Homoak for wrapping his small cigarettes, or knitting a band from bark string in anticipation of a death to which he must contribute such wealth.

Occasionally this pattern would be broken by some emergency requiring immediate action. This happened one morning to a man named Weyak, with whom I had become increasingly friendly, when he discovered that his watchtower had been knocked down by a disappointed enemy raiding party. They had come at dawn the day before to ambush Weyak or some of his companions, but it was cold and rainy and no one from Weyak's village wanted to go out. To show their scorn and to relieve their frustration, the enemy pulled down the tower.

The next day when Weyak saw what had happened, he began at once to rebuild it as quickly as possible, postponing all other tasks to do so. First he sent word to all the men who regularly spent their time guarding his tower. It was not really "his" tower; it was his responsibility because his gardens and those of the men from his village or of the men with whom he was closely related were nearest it.

Soon there were a dozen men on the little bluff above the Aikhé River where the tower, called Puakoloba or "place of yellow clay," lay ignominiously on the ground. A few men set about immediately to dig a new hole four or five feet deep into which the central mast of the tower would be set. Others went down to the river's edge to cut new vines to lash the lighter poles in place.

This activity began early in the morning; by midafternoon Puakoloba tower was resurrected, a few feet taller and much stronger than before. The hard work was done willingly and carefully. When it was finished, Weyak performed a little ceremony for which he had made a miniature bow and some tiny arrows; these he tucked into the lashings at the base of the tower facing the enemy. The toy weapons, together with a few handfuls of steamed grass placed on the ground around the tower, were meant to encourage the ghosts who helped those who guarded it and those who worked in gardens or strolled the paths nearby. Should anything happen near Puakoloba, it would not be because Weyak and his companions had not been diligent in their workmanship; nor would it be possible to find fault with the way it had been magically protected. Everyone went home late that afternoon pleased by what he had accomplished and confident that he had done it well.

2 Skills

The technology of the Dani is one of the simplest in the world. The tools are made of stone and bone, wood and bamboo. The raw materials are those of the local environment: wood, grass and vines. A few of the more exotic materials, such as sea shells, furs, feathers and the finest woods, reach the Grand Valley along native trade routes. Metals, and even pottery, were unknown to the Dani, and only in the few years since most of these photographs were taken has iron begun to be important in Dani technology. But despite their primitive tools, the houses and gardens of the Dani are complex and sophisticated.

p. 31 : **34.** Using a bone awl, a man weaves an ornamental wristband of pandanus fibers. The armbands of pigs' scrotums above his elbow are thought to ward off ghosts.

p. 31 : **35.** A man makes string from fibers beaten from the inner bark of various mountain bushes.

p. 31 : **36.** In casual moments men, using bone needles, weave the long cowrie shell bands which are exchanged at funerals. On his forehead the man is wearing an ornament of greased feathers.

p. 32 : **37.** A crude loom is sometimes used to weave bark string into strips on which snail shells are sewn for neck ornaments.

p. 32 : **38.** The Dani make fire by sawing a bamboo thong rapidly back and forth under a split hardwood stick. The friction creates embers which fall onto the tinder and ignite it. The whole process seldom takes more than a minute.

p. 32 : **39.** The gourds for men's penis sheaths are cultivated in gardens of the village compounds. The straight elongated shape results from weighting the end of the growing gourd with rocks. Sometimes a gourd is trained to bend or curve. Each man has a wardrobe of several sizes and shapes of gourds.

p. 32 : **40.** To make raincapes, girls gather reeds from fallow garden ditches and mat them into felted pads by jumping on them.

p. 32 : **41.** The felted cape provides women with some protection from the rain.

p. 32 : **42.** The Dani man's tool kit contains pig tusk scrapers, rodent tooth gravers, flint chips and greased fiber, all wrapped in banana "bark" and carried in a small net bag.

p. 32 : **43, 44.** In the long family house, one woman rolls fiber into string on her ash-whitened thigh, while another woman makes a carrying net.

p. 33 : **45.** A man splits firewood with a stone adze. The stone itself has been imported from a quarry some fifty miles to the northwest, but the hafting is done by the owner in the local style.

p. 33 : **46.** A young man uses a stone adze to sharpen the blade of his digging stick. Adzes are also used to chop down trees. Stone axes are rarer than adzes in this region and are used, if at all, only to split wood.

p. 33 : **47.** For a long time the Dani have sharpened their stone adzes and axes on bedrock outcroppings such as this one.

p. 33 : **48.** Limestone rocks and sand in a stream bed are used to shape and smooth a spear shaft. The finest spear woods are imported from distant valleys and only finished by the local people.

p. 33 : **49.** Just before a battle, a young man whitens the braided band on his spear with paste made from rotten limestone mixed with water.

p. 33 : **50.** Crude flint chips are used to make barbs on the hardwood tips of war arrows.

p. 33 : **51.** Men often soak their hair with charcoal-blackened pig grease for the sake of male beauty.

p. 33 : **52.** Sometimes a man greases and binds his hair in such a way that when it is released, he will have long regular curls.

p. 33 : **53.** Young men regularly wear feathers and shells, grease their faces and sometimes carry a bamboo mouth harp in a pierced ear lobe.

p. 33 : **54.** Spiders are collected in the forests and brought to the compounds, where they weave elaborate webs. These webs are compressed into magically protective strips which hang from the throat or, more rarely, are formed into hats.

p. 33 : **55.** Occasionally a man wears a tight cap of spiderweb ornamented with feathers and seeds.

p. 33 : **56.** Except when they are mourning or in ill health, Dani men pluck the hair from around their mouths.

Constructing a Pigsty

p. 34 : **57.** A man sets a center post by "throwing" it into the ground.

p. 34 : **58.** All Dani buildings are held together with only vine or bamboo thong lashings.

p. 34 : **59, 60.** The individual stalls of a pigsty are roofed with boards. They are held down by vines passed back and forth between men sitting on top and boys crouched in the stalls.

p. 34 : **61.** After the stalls are finished, the ridge pole is laid across the center poles.

p. 34 : **62.** Inside the sty each stall opens onto a common runway.

p. 34 : **63.** Before applying the thatch, branches are laid across roof slats to help anchor the grass.

Constructing a Woman's House

p. 35 : **64.** The center poles come up through the reed floor of the sleeping loft.

p. 35 : **65.** When finished, the sleeping loft is a warm, dark hemisphere heated through the cold nights by the hearth in the main lower room and by the bodies of the occupants. Personal belongings are kept in gourds and nets hung in the rafters.

p. 35 : **66, 67.** The dome is made of tall saplings stuck in the ground, bent over and lashed to the center posts and each other.

p. 35 : **68.** The lower room of the round house has walls of wooden planks and a low, narrow doorway.

p. 35 : **69.** In a new compound, a woman's house nears completion. Women make a mud base for a hearth in the sleeping loft. The thatch has been collected, and men prepare strips to attach the lowest layers.

Constructing a Family House

p. 36 : **70.** Two men use digging sticks to level the ground at the site of a new family house. The old family house, standing in the background, is too rotten to repair, but some of its lumber will be salvaged and used in building the new house.

p. 36 : **71.** The end walls are lashed and guide poles for positioning the side walls are laid down.

p. 36 : **72.** Pairs of uprights will hold the wall slats in place horizontally.

p. 36 : **73, 74.** Vines are used to lash the walls.

p. 36 : **75.** Boards are slipped between upright pairs.

p. 36 : **76.** Walls, center posts and ridge pole are now in place.

p. 36 : **77.** The roof framework is lashed in place.

p. 36 : **78.** Reeds are lashed to the roof slats as underthatch.

p. 36 : **79.** The long thatch grass is carefully laid.

p. 36 : **80.** A man trims the thatch by cutting it with a stone adze against a board held by another man.

p. 36 : **81.** An old family house is surrounded by taro, tobacco, banana and, growing over its roof, gourd vines.

Repairing a Watchtower

p. 37 : **82, 83.** Watchtowers stand along the perimeter of garden areas so that the no man's land beyond can be watched and enemy raids detected. Each watchtower is the responsibility of those men who have gardens in its immediate vicinity. Here a watchtower which was felled in an early-morning enemy raid is rebuilt. While some of the members of the watchtower group gather poles and vines, others begin to raise the first poles into place.

p. 37 : **84, 85.** The poles are lashed into a stable column with heavy vines.

p. 37 : **86.** As the younger men work on the watchtower, the older men relax in the shade of its shelter, smoking and gossiping, their spears close at hand.

p. 37 : **87.** During the day, while women work in the gardens, the men take turns as sentries in the tower.

Rock Drawings

p. 38 : **88–91.** For amusement, boys draw casual charcoal figures of people, garden plots, lizards and even ghosts on rock overhangs in the forest above the valley floor.

34

35

36

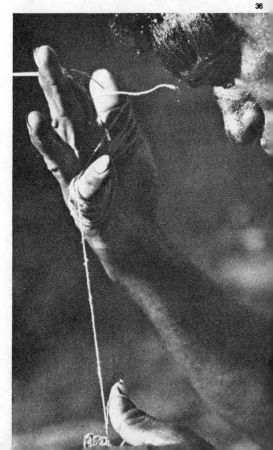

37

38

40

42

45
46
47
48
49
50
51
52
53
54
55
56

57 58 59 60

61 62 63

64 65 66

67 68

69

70

72

73

74

77

78

79

80

71

76

81

82

83

84

85

86

87

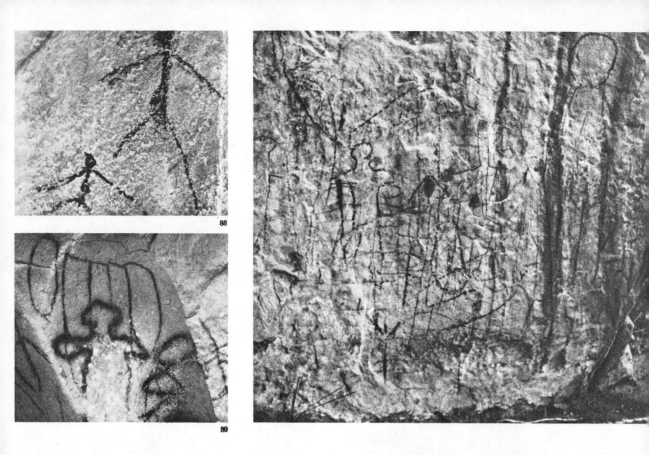

88

89

3 Nourishment

The Grand Valley of the Baliem includes not only the broad central plain but also the slopes and hills which climb up both sides to its high mountain walls. It is a vast and magnificently tended garden. In it the Dani spend most of their working lives, and from it they receive abundant and diverse nourishment.

The Dani have names for over seventy different kinds of sweet potatoes which are cultivated in the Baliem Valley. By the time a child is ten or twelve he recognizes most kinds by their blossom, vine and root. It seemed apparent that certain ones were preferred for breakfast, others for quick nourishment during work and still others for more relaxed eating in the evening. People at least had their preferences. Certainly we did, and the women who supplied us with sweet potatoes soon learned them and would bring our favorites on their way home from their gardens hoping that catering to our taste might mean a few more cowrie shells in exchange.

Since there are no seasons in the Baliem, agriculture is a continuous activity. The Dani are practically free from the kind of anxiety associated with other less fortunately situated farming cultures. Insufficient rain, floods or pests, which for seasonal planters could easily mean starvation, sometimes occur, but with considerably milder consequences. The Dani might lose some gardens to an enemy raiding party which, finding no one to kill, sometimes relieves its frustration by pulling up vines, but for the most part gardening is an uncomplicated if tedious routine.

In the Grand Valley, gardens may be on the plain or on the slopes. Where we stayed there were both types, since Wali's villages were situated between the hills and valley floor. The gardens on the hills behind the villages were simpler to plant and to maintain. Those in front of the villages on the flat valley floor were more complex in design; and from a height their intricate network of canals, which served both to irrigate and to drain the encircled plots, gave them a look of almost Byzantine elaboration. Slope land has virgin forest, though there is little land close to the villages which has not been cleared at least once. Usually the cover is short, dense brush, often including myrtle, laurel, rhododendron and even gardenia. The clearing is done by men using stone adzes to ring the larger trees which will eventually die. Later they return with sharpened digging sticks of hardened wood to root up the scrub. When a hillside garden is cleared and the sun has dried the brush, it is then burned. This may be done by women or men. The final step is terracing; this is considered heavy work, and women rarely participate.

The preparation of the gardens in the valley proper is hard work. There the ditches of old gardens must be cleared of the debris washed or thrown into them during the period of cultivation and harvest. A common sight was a cooperative work party of men and boys hip-deep in the ditches, carving great lumps of fertile muck from the bottom and tossing them onto the garden land to either side. They use long fire-hardened wood paddles which grow very heavy from the mud and water. From time to time a man will set his paddle aside and reach into the ditch for smaller lumps of mud which he plasters against the sides of the reshaped canal. This soon bakes dry in the sun and gives to these gardens a look of permanence and tidiness which lasts until they are abandoned to fallow.

The Dani are not happy at the prospect of hard work, but once they have begun, their mood is gay, not sullen. There is much laughter and joking among them, and their high spirits carry them through several hours of heavy labor. I have been told that the best opportunity for marital infidelity is during working hours. Villages are small and scarcely ever deserted, so lovers would almost surely be seen or heard by a child or an older person too feeble to work. But in the gardens, and particularly in the woods and thickets between or beyond them, men and women can meet with a reasonable certainty of being undiscovered. Discovery is most often made after the fact, when a woman declares she has been "raped," or when a man sees that his wife's attention has drifted to another man.

As soon as the ditches are scooped out, their banks sloped and plastered to prevent their erosion, and the beds between them cleared, the women and girls come to plant the sweet potatoes and other vegetables. All planting is done from cuttings taken from mature vines in the case of sweet potatoes, and with young plants in the case of taro. These are by no means the only vegetables cultivated. There is also ginger, yam, cucumber, banana and tobacco among other less important crops. A garden of sweet potatoes is planted in rows of individual mounds set approximately two feet apart. The only implement used is a sharpened stick about four feet long called *hipiri tegé* (sweet-potato spear). These sticks are virtually part of a woman's dress. She is never without one outside her village and never far from it in her own house. It is not only a tool but a weapon with which to defend herself if attacked or to belabor another woman with whom she might wish to quarrel. The spears are light, hard and highly polished from daily use. When planting, a hole is punched in the fresh soil for the cutting, which is then clamped in place by foot or hand. Until the cuttings begin to grow quite long the Dani give them little attention beyond

piling some dirt around them should the previous soil have been washed away by a particularly heavy rain. About three months after planting, the vines are pruned and the beds weeded. This period of cultivation continues for another three months, during which the mounds are covered with a mass of deep green leaf and flower and at the end of which they contain the first of perhaps a dozen mature roots.

Clearing ditches, planting, cultivating and harvesting goes on the year round; one month is as favorable for planting as another, for there is no summer or winter, nor dry or rainy period. The Dani must only be sure that as older gardens are harvested, others are being cultivated, planted and cleared.

There is seldom a day, unless it is miserably wet and cold or the occasion of an important religious ceremony, that Dani women do not spend several hours in their gardens. If the garden is in the valley, they must be sure that there are men in the watchtowers along the frontier. Usually the men of a village leave about an hour before the women, carrying only their weapons, some tobacco and perhaps a sweet potato to eat should they become hungry in the middle of the day. On reaching the watchtower, a man will put down his things and climb to its top; if he is alone and the first to arrive, he ascends to see better what activity is going on in neighboring gardens, especially in no man's land and beyond that in the gardens of the enemy half a mile away. If all is quiet, he or one of his tower companions will light a fire that serves to warm them, to light their cigarettes and to indicate that they will stay there. When the women leave their village, they look toward the frontier; if they see the smoke from their warrior's fire, they know that it is safe for them to proceed.

At the same time that the women leave for the gardens, the pigs which spend each night in the village also leave, usually under the care of a young boy or, more rarely, a young girl. Though it has minor significance as a source of nourishment, raising pigs does have a fascination and importance almost unequaled by any other activity in Dani society. As with sweet potatoes, it is not possible to date the introduction of domesticated pigs in the Baliem Valley, but it must be assumed that the idea of breeding and at least some of the values associated with the ownership and ritual use of these animals arrived as a unified concept. With many local differences of emphasis, this involvement in pigs is common throughout Melanesia.

The Dani consider pigs the most important living creatures besides people. They have both a fondness and respect for their natures. Pigs mean, above all else, wealth and social importance. To own a large herd is the most desirable of all goals. Only the possession of several wives is as important, and usually a man who has many pigs will have more than one wife, for it is pigs which provide a man with the economic and social leverage that enables him to attract and hold together a polygamous household.

Whereas the ownership and use of pigs are almost exclusively a male prerogative, their care falls most heavily upon women and children. A man, it would seem, is as much interested in having wives and children to look after his pigs as he is in having the animals in order to afford wives and children. Ordinarily a man will look after only the most important matters relating to the care and handling of his pigs. He will decide which are to be given at a funeral of a close relative, which are to be fattened and then given away at the important periodic religious ceremonies, and which are to be donated as small or sometimes orphaned animals to a child or wife. A man also supervises the breeding of his stock, and assures selective breeding by castrating all but the best males. On one occasion Weyak rose from his usual sweet-potato breakfast and in the courtyard of Homaklep called to his two wives to bring a certain pig. With considerable commotion the pig was caught and hung by its hind legs face inward to the courtyard fence. Using a bamboo knife, with two deft incisions, Weyak exposed the animal's testes, and with two more strokes excised them. Then he took two pieces of supple grass and sutured the incisions, packed some wet ash on the wound, and released the still-shrieking pig. The severed parts were brought into the men's house, briefly roasted and eaten.

Less important chores connected with raising Dani pigs are left to women and children. They are really closest to the animals which are their day-to-day responsibility. First they must accompany the pigs when they leave the village in the morning to root in the fallow gardens. Inevitably, the young herders will relieve this otherwise tiresome task with a variety of games. When they do, a pig sometimes strays and is lost, or falls into a garden ditch to drown, or, rarest of all, is stolen by someone passing by. These are calamitous occasions, and the owner is often cruel in treating the offending guardian.

Because they are important in economic terms, pigs enjoy a protected status in the Dani world. For the same reason, however, there are frequent attempts made to acquire pigs by either stealth or subterfuge. Most stealing goes on between men of distant villages who usually have female scores to settle. In sufficient numbers, pigs can pacify a husband whose wife left him for another man. The reason for taking the animals might be that the man who has acquired the new woman is not convinced that she is worth his pigs. In such a situation, the male relatives and friends of the aggrieved husband will visit the village where the woman has gone to live. The controversy will be well known to everyone since such disputes constitute one of the most important matters of social interaction and hence will have been discussed at length by hundreds of people over a wide area. If the visiting party is sufficiently strong, they may be met only by innocent bystanders, the offender and his friends having fled. Under such circumstances, the visitors will simply round up a herd of pigs belonging to the man who has their woman and drive them back to their own village. Sometimes, however, the party seeking redress is neither large nor politically important enough to intimidate its adversary. This happens when the forsaken husband has few relatives or is himself weak, poor and inconsequential. The Dani have a word for such people, *kepu*, and though it has many subtle meanings, in essence it signifies worthlessness. A true *kepu* would probably have no wife to steal— or if he did, no one would want her. Someone unillustrious and lacking kith or kin, however, might easily meet with further humiliation and disgrace by seeking redress.

Of course there are infinite variations on this theme of vengeance in the valley, and civil order is maintained by a balance between strength of arms and traditional payments in pigs or other wealth in amounts and in a manner decided by particular circumstances.

In the domain of subsistence, the Dani are most active in agriculture and most fond of pig breeding. There is another activity which ranks with farming and herding in importance, if not in scale: the making of salt. Salt is not only an essential item of diet, it is also a prominent feature of a complex trade system.

The economic life of the Grand Valley Dani is not limited merely to subsistence activities such as sweet potato gardening and the domestication of pigs. Their material needs are more varied than that. Their technology is termed neolithic only because of their dependence on stone tools. The Baliem is basically an area of limestone, and the more durable stone necessary for making axes and adzes is situated in deposits well beyond the boundaries of specifically Dani culture. There are, in fact, quarries some fifty or so miles to the north, where a linguistically related but politically unaffiliated group lives and manufactures stone implements for surrounding social and cultural groups. These tools are traded to the Dani for goods that the quarry people in turn lack or desire in greater abundance.

One of the natural resources within the Dani area is the salt well of Iluerainma. This is really a system of briny pools, famous because much of the Valley depends for its salt on this place high up the eastern wall not far north of Wali's neighborhood. The salt prepared from these pools gives the Dani their leverage in trade arrangements with surrounding communities. As long as the Dani control the pools at Iluerainma, and as long as they are industrious in exploiting the valuable contents, they will have access to stone tools, various woods no longer growing in the Baliem needed for weapons, the feathers of birds of paradise, which inhabit higher and more forested country to the east, and of course shells, which make their way from both shores of New Guinea to the very heart of the Central Highlands by an elaborate and unknown trading network.

Sometimes women go to the salt wells simply to satisfy their own domestic needs, and it was with this intention that Laka, one of Weyak's wives, one afternoon chopped down a mature banana plant behind her husband's men's house. It was a tall, treelike plant that had already borne its bunch of bananas and therefore was to be turned to other uses. When the stalk had fallen,

Laka and three or four young girls in the village took their digging sticks and began to peel the outer sheaths of the pulpy trunk. They then cut the leaves away and chopped the branches and the trunk into lengths of about three feet. Much effort was spent on pressing the sap from the banana plant segments, using the digging stick as a combination rolling pin and draw plane. This treatment made the layers of trunk and branches limp and more absorbent.

The next morning Laka and her daughters, along with another woman and her daughters, tied the prepared banana trunk into soggy bundles and set forth to Iluerainma. Their route took them north along what the members of our expedition called the "salt trail" because so many people used it to carry this commodity up and down the valley. The weight of each load was immense—between fifty and one hundred pounds, depending on the age and strength of the carrier. It is a long way from Wali's neighborhood to the wells—perhaps five miles, the last half mile being a steep climb up the eastern mountain wall along a rocky trail often as slippery as ice from the forest dampness.

At the wells there is a clearing where people who have come from all directions sit to rest or wait while their banana tree segments are soaking in the pools. Usually the women do more pounding and pulping at the pools to be sure that as much as possible of the briny water is soaked up. This is almost exclusively women's work, though occasionally one sees an old man filling gourds and long bamboo containers by submerging them in the pools. Though there is great activity at Iluerainma, there is a curious absence of sociability. All the women working there go about their tasks with a deliberateness which suggests that they have no desire to tarry or gossip, as they might in their own gardens or along the paths between their villages. The reason is that people are drawn to Iluerainma from many different and distant areas. Though nearly all of them are Dani, and though they all speak closely related dialects, the salt well is home territory only to those whose villages lie close by. Anyone else who comes is a visitor, and their safe passage to and from the well depends on the state of relations between them, other visitors and the people who live nearby.

When Laka and her companions emerged from the well, they began immediately to make up the burdens of soggy banana plant to be transported back down the mountain wall. This done, we left the well without a word spoken to anyone; while we were there, groups came and went silently in all directions.

Our path went straight down the wall, the pace set by the loping stride of the women who led the way. With every step their mood brightened, despite the immense cargo of dripping banana pulp which hung down in overlapping nets from their heads. At the foot of the wall the trail debouches on the open valley near one of Kurelu's villages. Here we stopped for a moment to rest before resuming the long march across gardens and slippery poles that spanned the innumerable ditches and rivers between Iluerainma and Laka's village several miles to the south.

By late afternoon the salt excursion was over. Laka and Milige put their soggy nets into their houses for the night. The next day they would be emptied and the strips of banana pulp hung on the fences or draped on the thatched roofs to dry in the sun. A few days later the pulp would be burned to ash and gathered into two or three round packages enclosed in green banana leaves. These hard, salty balls would be used up or traded and within a few weeks there would be another trip to the wells.

3 Nourishment

The food of the Dani is primarily sweet potato. Baked in the coals or steamed in a leaf bundle, the sweet potato is eaten by every Dani several times a day and constitutes at least ninety percent of his diet. The rest of his fare is made up of other tubers, as well as pork, greens and fruit. Seasoning is seldom used, but occasionally salt is sprinkled onto meat, and once or twice a year a man makes a sauce from the red pandanus fruit. Meals are monotonous but satisfying. No Dani ever starves, except for those who live along the banks of the Baliem itself, where gardens are occasionally flooded. Partly because of the low birth rate, partly because of the war deaths, there is as yet no population pressure in the Grand Valley.

p. 47 : **92.** Men's cooperative work teams scoop up the rich silt that has settled in the irrigation ditches and spread it over the garden beds at planting time.

p. 48 : **93–95.** Firmer ditch mud is sliced by paddle-shaped digging sticks so that it can be lifted onto the garden beds. The digging sticks are made of wood which has been hardened in fire.

p. 48 : **96.** Weeds which have filled the ditches since the last planting are thrown onto the garden beds as compost.

p. 48 : **97.** After the heavy work of opening the garden is finished, a man retires to the watchtower shelter and his wife plants the sweet-potato cuttings.

p. 49 : **98.** A woman works in her sweet-potato gardens while a man sits in the watchtower, guarding against an enemy raid.

p. 49 : **99.** A work team of men, gathered in a friend's garden, turns the sod with heavy fire-hardened digging sticks.

p. 49 : **100.** A woman, her body smeared with yellow clay, in mourning for a recently dead relative, cultivates immature taro and sweet-potato plants.

p. 49 : **101.** After men prepare the ground, women plant sweet-potato cuttings with their light digging sticks.

p. 50 : **102.** The harvested sweet potatoes are washed before cooking.

p. 51 : **103.** A mother and daughter, returning from their gardens, climb through the entrance in the outer fence of their compound.

p. 51 : **104.** The job of clearing and burning off the light vegetation from gardens is left to the women.

p. 51 : **105.** Wrapping coals which she has brought from home in grass, a woman blows them into flame to make a garden fire.

p. 51 : **106, 107.** On the mountain slopes flanking the Grand Valley, gardens are made by cutting down all but the largest trees and burning off the debris.

p. 51 : **108, 109.** A woman plants sweet potatoes in one of the more established treeless slope gardens.

Raising Pigs

p. 52 : **110.** Domestic pig meat is the majour source of Dani protein, and pig exchange and feasting form the core of every Dani ceremony. Pigs spend the night in their stalls, where they are sometimes attacked by rats. In the morning, before taking the pigs to root in old gardens, women treat these wounds with pitch and ash.

p. 52 : **111.** Alongside the high main entrance in the compound fence, there is another entrance at ground level which can be opened for pigs.

p. 52 : **112.** Each pig has a name, and before they are finally slaughtered in a ceremony the larger animals are almost members of the family.

p. 52 : **113.** Before the mist has lifted from the mountain wall, a boy takes two pigs for their day in a fallow garden.

Salt Preparation

p. 53 : **114.** In the first step in salt preparation, the women and girls of a compound cut up and dry strips from the trunk of a banana plant.

p. 53 : **115.** Near the salt pool a woman beats the parts of the banana stem before putting it in the pool to soak.

p. 53 : **116.** Women squeeze the banana strips as they soak in the brine.

p. 53 : **117.** After the brine-soaked strips have dried in the sun, women and girls reduce them to ash.

p. 53 : **118.** After collecting a pile of ashes on fresh banana leaves, a girl wets it and then ties it into a bundle. These hard balls of salty ash are used for seasoning food; they also are an important item of trade for the people of the neighborhood.

p. 54 : **119.** The brine pool of Iluerainma lies beside a stream high above the Grand Valley. It is the major source of salt for all the Dani.

Color Section

p. 55 : **120.** Men clear a garden ditch, throwing fertile compost onto the sweet-potato beds.

p. 55 : **121.** Sweet-potato cuttings are planted two to a mound.

p. 55 : **122.** Whenever men leave their village they carry weapons.

p. 55 : **123.** Women burn the dry brine-soaked banana trunk to make a salty ash.

p. 55 : **124.** The irrigation ditches of the sweet-potato gardens form a watery labyrinth.

p. 55 : **125.** A woman carries her garden produce in nets hanging down her back suspended from the top of her head.

p. 55 : **126.** After the brine-soaked banana trunk is reduced to ash, it is packed into a banana leaf bundle.

p. 55 : **127.** A woman on the way to her gardens in the early morning carries hot coals for her fire.

p. 55 : **128.** Colorful parrot feathers are used for a headband.

p. 55 : **129.** A girl herds pigs.

p. 55 : **130.** A boy cuts ripe bananas with a stone adze.

p. 55 : **131.** A boy smells a fragrant rhododendron.

p. 55 : **132.** A woman brings firewood home.

p. 55 : **133.** A stone adze is used to butcher a pig.

p. 55 : **134.** A man slices the red pandanus fruit with a pig bone knife.

p. 55 : **135.** A hawk.

p. 55 : **136.** A woman weeds her garden with a digging stick.

p. 55 : **137.** Men use pig grease and ashes to improve their looks.

p. 55 : **138.** The first stage in the construction of a round men's house is the erection of wall planks.

p. 55 : **139.** A grandmother trims the edge of a new reed skirt for her granddaughter.

pp. 56–57 : **140.** Away from the fighting, an army masses prior to entering battle.

p. 58 : **141.** At a funeral a mourning girl is decorated with many colors of clay.

p. 59 : **142.** A girl who has had her fingers chopped off on the second day of a funeral watches the women distribute nets brought as gifts.

pp. 60–61 : **143.** Men and women dance to celebrate the killing of an enemy.

p. 62 : **144.** Boys learn to kill by playing spear-the-hoop, a game whose object is to throw a toy spear through a rolling, bouncing vine hoop.

p. 62 : **145.** Their arrows and spears ready, two sides face each other in formal battle.

93

94

95

96

97

103

104

105

106

107

108

109

110

111

112

113

114

115

116

117

118

4 Play

By the very clarity and simplicity of its expression, the play of children is often an excellent window through which an observer may look upon a culture otherwise concealed by complexities, suspicion and the barriers of language. This is particularly true of the *jegerugui,* the children of the Dani. Because of the exigencies to which they are born, these children can afford to lose no time growing up. When the boys are four or five they begin to join somewhat older boys in a variety of games which help prepare them to take part in the formal warfare organized by their elders. The girls, who are not as free as the boys, spend less time at play; at a very early age their energy is channeled into the purposeful pursuits of female life. Long before boys begin to behave like men, girls are little women—planting, cultivating, cooking and doing a great variety of other more complicated tasks. They mature more quickly both because they must and because it is in their nature to do so. Still, while

they are children they are not without some childish pleasures. Occasionally they even compete with their male contemporaries and, being girls, are more than able to hold their own, playing at war with little cane spears and short grass darts. More often they play among themselves or with their smaller brothers, whom they often care for during the day. During such times they make little villages of grass and twigs, plant toy gardens and weave tiny skirts about their fists. Their world, when it is not real, is full of pretend. But for girls the reality is far more demanding of their time than it is for boys of the same age.

This is not to say that a boy spends his childhood dreaming of feckless fun; much depends on the individual's situation. Young boys who have no brothers or sisters of approximately the same age in their immediate household must work at jobs that by custom fall to the young. Such tasks include the important and time-consuming responsibility of watching the family herd of pigs while they root about an abandoned garden. The boys must collect wood for the fires that are always burning in the several houses of each village, fetch water in long bamboo tubes or bottles made from dried and hollowed gourds and run errands of all sorts for some older person. A child's life, even that of the favored boy, is not an easy one. Children are cold for part of every day, especially in the early morning, when they must leave the warmth of their houses to take the pigs from their stalls and herd them to the fields. They are comfortable during most of the day but cold again in the evening before they lie down on the sleeping platform above the fire in the men's house or the women's house. Children are also frequently hurt, either by being rebuked and punished by their elders or because their still-tender skins are almost completely naked and hence vulnerable.

The Dani use two words to distinguish one sort of game from another: *negal-negal* means "pretend" and refers to games of little consequence; and *yelé* means more precisely "play" and refers to games of some seriousness. Often the Dani convey the essential childishness of what they are discussing by simply repeating a word. For example, a long purple flower attached to a bark string and pulled about by a child is called *wam-wam*—pig-pig.

All children's activity (apart from the tasks they are called upon to do by their elders) by no means falls neatly into the category of serious play or idle fun. Most games are fun whether serious or not; the distinction has more meaning for someone watching than for anyone playing. Only when a boy gets hit in the eye by an undetected grass dart—as frequently happens while playing *weem yelé* does a child take a more sober view of what he is doing. In the midst of tears he may well regret that the game he is

playing must be so rough, and he will probably be reluctant to take an active part next time. However, the great majority of such casualties never stop playing completely. There are several warriors who fight in the front lines during full-scale battles with one milky eye that was blinded by a grass spear in childhood.

Having neither schools nor any other kind of formal teaching, the Dani must transmit their culture to the young in other ways. The children learn by watching and listening. They are schooled by direct contact with virtually all the major events of life by the time they are five years old. They know about magic, death, war, gardening, house building and pig keeping by having experienced them. Very little is hidden from children, and of course it is in everyone's interest that he knows how things are done. There are taboos which are supposed to prevent certain children from eating certain things or from going certain places, but these are also meant to prepare them for life by keeping them strong and well.

Children also teach each other through their games. They learn to be warriors not only by listening to men talk about wars, but by having their own *weem yelés*, or war games. Just as *weem yelé* gives young boys practice in dodging arrows, so does *sigogo wasin* give them a chance to perfect their aim with spears. *Sigogo wasin* means "kill the hoop," and the game is aptly named. Two groups of players separated by about twenty-five yards alternately throw and spear a hoop of twisted cane that rolls and bounces past them as they wait, poised, with their toy spears. A hoop is "killed" when it has been pierced in flight and nailed to the ground. Boys, and sometimes girls, play this game often until the swallows come to dance in the twilight air.

Another game, which trains its participants to appreciate the more brutal aspects of war, is played with the ripened seeds of the tall pitto-sporum. A pair of boys will gather several hand-fuls of the little pea-sized seeds—enough to make two opposing armies—and then they take turns throwing a sharpened stick the length of a pencil into their opponent's army of seed-men. Each player has one throw before giving up the stick to his adversary. The object is to skewer the soft-coated seed with the little spear and thereby to kill an enemy warrior. When this occurs, the "dead man" is taken off the field and put away from the battle. To the accompaniment of battle noises which each boy continually mumbles, the seeds are maneuvered all about the little battle-field.

There is great realism in this game, and even more in another game closely related to it. Since most deaths on both sides occur during raids, there is a game designed to fix the importance of alertness in a child's mind. Children play with toy watchtowers manned by the same type of seed used in the battle game. The seed in the watchtower is ambushed by a small and stealthy band of raiding seeds that sneak up on the sleepy sentry and knock him from his tower. In real life this sort of raid is extremely dangerous, since watchtowers are usually guarded by more than a single lookout and the raiding party must always be small enough to remain unseen. Such raids are successful only through a combination of defensive folly and offensive surprise, and so the victorious raiding party has special reasons for exultation.

As they play at sudden death, the children are learning important facts of life. If kill-the-hoop and various games of war are part of a child's education in violent behavior, o-o sili and sili-eken are instructive in other, more peaceful as-pects of Dani life. Boys and girls can be involved in both games, since the first (which means "wood-wood village") is really what we know as "playing house." The only difference is that the young Dani play "village." That is, sili-eken (literally "village seeds") is played by several children who collaboratively outline an entire village, including fences and homes, with the flat and pointed araucaria seeds. Their villages of seeds are also idealized replicas of what these children so often see when they look down at their compounds from the fields and gardens high on the mountain wall.

Due to their family circumstances, some children must find or invent games that can be played alone. Pua is the little swineherd who lives in Wubarainma, the only small child of his mother, Ogonege. Nearly every day Pua spends several morning and afternoon hours with his pigs. Other children may be herding a few hundred yards away, but neither Pua nor they are free to give their time and attention to play while they watch their pigs. Even so, they do play, if only by themselves. One day Pua began to play a game which he called mokat asuk, "ghost ear." This is a good example of child's magic. He made a little cave, about the size of his own head, in the side of a small hill, in which he put the top of a particularly fleshy and remark-ably convoluted mushroom. The mushroom—the ghost ear—looked astonishingly real and dead. Across the opening he placed twigs and leaves to seal up the entrance. He would leave the ear for a time, hoping that when he returned it would have heard news of his dead father and be able to tell him where he was and how he felt.

Another solitary game, perhaps even invented by Pua, is tegebok, a game which can be played only when the ground is damp. It consists of shaping little saucers of mud and then throwing them down on a piece of flat ground; the trapped air inside bursts through the mud dish making a loud crack much like that of an empty Dixie Cup stamped under foot.

In short, most of the activity of Dani children may be called play, for it does not contribute directly to the adults' activities. But it is educational. Before a Dani child is old enough to take his full place in society, he has acted out in his games most of the adult activities—has in fact practiced the skills of adulthood. In a society which lacks schools, such play has great importance.

In addition to the skills and techniques which he will use as an adult, the child also learns the attitudes of his culture. It is very striking that Dani games are not competitive, and rarely is there a winner. Even in a game such as spear-the-berry, scores are not kept, and the children usually tire of it before one side is victorious. This absence of direct competition is found in adult life as well; competition is muted and there are few measurable standards of achievement, goals or titles for which men strive. Skill and cooperation are more important than competition, both in games and in life itself.

Art is almost irrelevant in Dani life. There is considerable craftsmanship in their tools, dwellings and gardens, and much that is decorative in their use of shells and feathers, but art for its own sake is rare.

The Dani do possess a type of cave art, consisting of crude designs drawn in charcoal on overhanging rock faces. These rock shelters are scattered throughout the forests behind the villages and afford shelter to wood gatherers or hunters caught by one of the frequent sudden showers. The men make a fire with the bamboo thongs they carry on such expeditions, and sit out the storm, talking, smoking their native tobacco and perhaps knitting on a shell band. During this time boys will take a chunk of charcoal from the edge of the fire and draw figures on the smooth areas of the rocky overhangs. They make men and women, trees, birds, sala-

manders, garden beds and even ghosts. But this is little more than doodling, for the designs are simple, casually done and quickly forgotten.

There are, however, some rock drawings of a very different sort, hidden on nearly inaccessible cliffs away from the villages. These are made by men during the boys' initiation ceremony and show human hands, X's and crescents, all in red. They are reminiscent of prehistoric art in many other parts of the world. The human hand is one of the common designs of the earliest art of every continent, and the color red is a frequent symbol in initiation rites. Sometimes, as with the Dani, it is a red ocher, but often it is the red of a boy's blood.

It is hard to say why the Dani are such avid craftsmen and decorators but not artists. To say that they spend their time on war instead of art is insufficient, for many cultures which wage war also produce great art. In fact, when war is as important to ritual (as is Dani war), it often inspires art. However, this is not the case in the Grand Valley of the Baliem.

The Dani sing. This may be a cultural universal: just as all cultures have language, so do all have songs. The several types of Dani songs include adult songs, those of the funeral and those of victory. Sometimes these songs have simple lyrics, almost prayers; sometimes they are only meaningless sounds. Usually one man sings a lead and is answered by the chorus of all others present. Harmony seems to be accidental. These songs are reserved for more or less serious, formal circumstances of ritual, or are used to greet a man who has not been seen for a long time. These group songs are never accompanied by musical instruments, for the Dani have none but the bamboo mouth harp. Men and boys make these harps and play them quietly when they are alone or sitting at the edge of a group. They emit a pleasant, unobtrusive twang and drone. (Often men sit alone and preoccupied, grinding their molars together. Fearsome as this may seem, for the Dani it connotes a gentle purr of contentment.)

The boys have little songs, sung to one or two standard tunes, with regular form and complex words. These melodies may evoke the beauties of nature or involve sexually obscene puns. These two themes are peculiar, since neither seems to figure prominently in ordinary Dani conversation. Such tunes are sung with great exuberance and humor. It would be very difficult to translate one in all its richness, but the following examples give an idea of this form:

"I shall go far away, I shall go far away,"
You were saying long ago.
Giluge girl, Yaiige girl.
You are sitting close to the hearth.
"I shall go far away, I shall go far away,"
You were saying long ago.
Giluge girl, Yaiige girl.

You are sitting next to the poles of the fireplace.
I don't want to buy nassa shells,
I don't want to buy cowrie shells.
Giluge girl, Yaiige girl.
The blue sky up there, your hand grasped it,
The white cloud down there, your foot stepped
   on it.

We walk up the gentle slope [to look around].
What is it that is not eaten?

Here [come] the Wio people,
Here [come] the Dolimo people.
Here I'll look for salt,
Here I'll look for trade salt.
The dark leaves of the *wigi* trees are good,
   let's go.
The light leaves of the *bakho* tree are good,
   let's go.
Where Nilik sits, there are fighting arrows,
   let's go.
Where Elaborok sits, there are fighting arrows,
   let's go.

4 Play

p. 71 : **146.** To pass the time, some young children throw a net into the air. If it is caught, they cry **werak** (boy), but if they miss, they cry **hodlak** (girl). This is a very casual game, played by younger children. It has little significance, and no one feels bad about missing.

p. 72 : **147.** Boys build play houses in the long savanna grass while herding pigs. The play houses imitate those which their fathers build, with a lashed reed frame covered over with grass thatch. They are used for a few hours and then abandoned to the wind and rain.

p. 72 : **148.** Grass arches are tied by the children in the open fields, but they are reminiscent of magical arches used in garden and curing ceremonies. The children say it is **weligat** ("for no particular reason").

p. 72 : **149.** A boy draws circles in the sand by pivoting his foot. The designs represent pig tails which are cut off during funeral ceremonies and then displayed to placate the ghosts. Lines drawn through the circle represent a pig's tail, and the circle itself is the large patch of skin cut off with the tail.

p. 72 : **150.** A boy amuses himself by throwing mud saucers over a hole in the ground. His shoulders are smeared with mud, imitating the epaulettes of the small bird of the immortality myth.

p. 72 : **151.** A cat's-cradle string game, similar to those found all over the world, is played by an unmarried girl. Most boys and girls know several of these string games. Some of them simply form designs; others act out little stories.

p. 72 : **152.** A married woman's skirt, or **yogal,** made of sedge stalks is wound on a girl's hand. The girl herself will wear the hanging skirt until the day of her marriage, when a real **yogal** will be wound around her waist. When this girl was younger, several of her fingers were chopped off to placate the ghosts.

p. 73 : **153.** The bamboo mouth harp is the only common Dani musical instrument. Men and boys make their own and strum them at odd moments.

p. 73 : **154.** Boys play simple flutes by blowing across the top of a reed.

p. 73 : **155.** A vibrating bamboo bow thong gives a small boy practice in mouthing the sounds which he will eventually make on a mouth harp.

p. 74 : **156.** A father demonstrates the use of a toy bow and arrow to his son.

p. 75 : **157–159.** Kill-the-seed is one of the mock battle games played by boys too young to fight. The opposing berry armies are moved back and forth in charges and retreats. In detailed imitation of adult life, a seed warrior is placed in the twig watchtower and then removed when his army retreats.

pp. 76–79 : **160–165.** Kill-the-hoop **(sigogo wasin),** played by boys and even girls in abandoned fields, sharpens their skill with spears. One group of children bounces a vine hoop past the other group, who try to impale it with their toy spears.

pp. 80–85 : **166–177.** In another battle game, groups of boys imitate their elders, charging back and forth and throwing heavy grass-stem spears at each other. This teaches throwing and dodging skills, as well as battle strategy.

p. 86 : **178.** A boy uses toy bows and arrows to stalk and kill small songbirds, which are roasted and eaten. For the Grand Valley Dani, hunting is more a boys' pastime than a food-gathering activity.

147

148

149

150

151

153

154

155

157

158

159

[75]

160

161

162

167

168

170

169

171

175

176

5 Ghosts

No phenomenon, either real or imagined, is of greater significance to Dani life than their belief in ghosts. The logic of their existence rests on the premise that all happenings are the result of both human and ghostly instrumentality. Like magnetism or gravity, ghostliness is not itself visible except through its manifestations. When a person falls while walking on a path that a recent rain has made greasy with mud, he will often say that a ghost made him slip, and though he might also say that he saw the ghost, he would not claim that he saw how it had made him fall.

The presence of ghosts is as real to every Dani as the company of his family and friends. They dwell in his world with the same certainty and conclusiveness as any other living creature. Ghosts, in fact, are "living" dead. They are the shades of deceased relatives and friends, the insubstantial survivors of the intermediate crisis of death. They are thought to possess all the faculties of a living person plus certain special attributes and qualities deriving from their incorporeality. They both walk and fly, eat sweet potatoes and make rain, understand human speech and shoot invisible arrows. They are powerful, though not omnipotent in the sense that the living must passively accept their domination.

The Dani do not separate themselves from ghosts through fear or ignorant superstition; ghosts constitute one of the most essential and continually experienced realities of their lives. In essence, ghosts are no more than privileged humans, refined by death. They are more demanding, more hungry, more inquisitive and more vindictive than they were in life. These are familiar traits to every Dani, and so the way that people live with ghosts is largely an extension of the way in which they live with one another.

Still, ghosts have certain advantages, which means that in maintaining good relations with them, one must employ magic as well as practicality. Because ghosts are not completely predictable, it is often hard for a man to know on just how good terms he is with them. His family, friends and enemies can be seen and judged by their looks or behavior, but it is safest to assume that ghosts are never wholly satisfied, that whatever has been done to please them is either not quite enough, or must be repeated to be effective.

It is for these reasons that the Dani hold frequent magical ceremonies; without in any sense being cowed or awed by the imagined power of ghosts, they sprinkle much of their casual day-to-day behavior with ritual or magical acts. As with all people, primitive or civilized, it is difficult at first to detect the magical forms of behavior, for no sharp line is drawn by the Dani between magical behavior and what might seem normal to others. For example, when a Dani eats a banana he will, without giving a thought to his act, put the skin in the rafters of his house so that it will dry and can later be burned. He does this because he believes that his stomach would have swollen up had he thrown the skin into the weeds or gardens around the village. Magic in association with bananas does not end here. For example, it is taboo for anyone of a certain kinship group to eat certain types of bananas, though even so clear a rule as this is broken on occasion. Whether banana peels are properly disposed of or eaten, if the person is of that group, probably depends on what sort of rapport exists between an individual and the ghosts at any particular moment.

A Dani's concern about ghosts is more often

expressed in a desire that they "stay where they belong," that they "do not come around bothering us." The ideal relationship between living persons and ghosts, which one might call the goal of Dani ritual, is marked by both physical separation and mutual respect. If the living perform the appropriate ceremonies, they expect the ghosts to keep their distance. But, like most other ideals, this one is never fully realized. Within the logic which they have developed to explain such things, the Dani understand that the ghosts are greedier and more meddlesome than they ought to be, and they themselves are too often willing to neglect their magical duties and obligations. How else could they explain the repeated occurrence of sickness, bad weather and, most frequent of all, a sort of spiritual malaise? This last is not so much an infirmity as a condition, like the nasal drip that afflicts so many Dani in a kind of tidal rhythm throughout their lives. Their spiritual condition is judged poor or healthy by reference to imaginary matter located at the solar plexus. They are called the *etai-eken,* or "seeds of singing," and correspond roughly to both our concepts of the soul and of personality. They are sometimes associated with the physiological heart, though in addition they have supernatural qualities. All creatures possess this indispensable ingredient, with the exception of insects and reptiles. In humans, however, these "seeds" have a significance surpassing that of all other elements of one's constitution, and are closely related, at the very foundation of Dani metaphysics, to their equally important concept of a world in part controlled by ghosts.

A Dani baby is born with the promise of his share of the human allotment of "seeds of singing," but he is not thought to truly possess them until about six months after birth. At that time it is believed that they appear in the child's back, close to the spinal column. Henceforth, until the child is capable of sensible speech, the rudimentary seeds develop in size and shift toward the solar plexus. From a very young age the *etai-eken* are regarded by every individual as the most essential part of his being, their vital center, combining the attributes of both heart and soul. For this reason they are anxiously watched and protected. Having appeared in infancy at the backbone, the *etai-eken* are known to retreat under terrible stress to their original site. When this happens every effort must be made to replace them in their proper position, just under the peak of the rib's archway, where healthy and properly located *etai-eken* can be seen throbbing just beneath the skin. There are other dangers to be avoided or corrected. Sometimes a man's *etai-eken* turn over and fail to function normally upside down. They are also known to crumple or collapse as if, like any other neglected seed, they had withered or shriveled. In all events, no matter what the specific distress, the victim knows that the ghosts are somehow implicated, if not directly responsible.

One of the most dramatic expressions of the interplay between forces that affect the well-being of the living is in intertribal hostilities. When a member of one warring faction has been killed by his enemy, there is set in motion an elaborate sequence of events whose purpose is to kill a person on the offending side. However, the motive is not simply revenge. Nor do these people enjoy killing for its own sake. Instead, there is a complex process of reasoned behavior that occurs between deaths, and leads to the inevitable climax of another killing. When a person has been killed, the village of the deceased immediately starts funeral preparations. On the day following death the corpse is cremated in a large public ceremony, and for another four days the traditional rites accorded death are performed. During this period, beginning with the moment when the corpse is laid on the fire and his ghost is released, all people connected with the deceased must assume a special role in relation to the new-made ghost. It is axiomatic in Dani reasoning that such a ghost will not rest until the living avenge it. Its unrest is the principal concern of its living relatives and associates, for the ghost turns to them for satisfaction. The often-stated desire that the ghosts "go away and leave us alone" is never an antidote to the interfering demands of a fresh and unavenged ghost.

But the funeral rites are only part of the whole pattern of appeasement which must eventually include the taking of an enemy life. The pressure that ghostly powers put upon their living relatives is felt to be a weakening or disarrangement of one's *etai-eken*. Since well-being is measured in terms of the condition of the *etai-eken*, almost as we employ the notion of body temperature or fever, and since any disturbances in their function have not physical but also grave spiritual conse-quences, a way has to be found to restore damaged *etai-eken* to good health. In fact, there are many cures, and one is chosen according to the character and circumstances of a particular ailment. A death at the hands of an enemy de-mands more radical and comprehensive treat-ment than anything else, since it is an affair that threatens the well-being of the entire group.

On the other hand, a wounded warrior, especially if his injury is not too serious, must suffer alone; only he can take steps to protect himself from possible adversity stemming from ghostly interference. Ordinary sickness, when it shows any sign of becoming chronically or pro-gressively debilitating, is often blamed on either ghosts or witchcraft. In either case, and despite the specific nature of the symptoms, victims eval-uate their state of health as much by the imagi-nary condition of their *etai-eken* as by the amount of real pain or distress they may be suffering.

On virtually all occasions when ghosts are suspected of being the cause of trouble of any kind, a magical formula is already available or can be quickly devised to counteract their efforts. If, for example, it rains on the afternoon of some important gathering—such as a funeral to which many people have come from a long distance to grieve and talk and eat—a man, confident of his right to express himself boldly, will tell the ghosts to go away in words such as these: "You ghosts, wave your hands and chase the rain away. You should be ashamed. You have been well treated. Dry the rain up and go to your homes."

The ghosts' homes are generally about a half mile from most villages at places called *mokat ai;* there, after the corpse is burned, his ghost is meant to live with other ghosts from the same village. But since ghosts do not stay where they belong, but come around the villages and gardens for a variety of reasons, usually malicious, other structures are built in places they are known to frequent. In every *sili,* which is really a segment of a compound village, there is a small wooden structure with four sides and two compartments within. On one side is a tiny doorway through which the ghosts are meant to come and go. It is periodically repaired and refurbished to provide a resting place for wandering ghosts; the Dani do so only because their efforts to keep them away from villages is never wholly successful.

Another frequently encountered structure is found both in gardens and around certain vil-lages. Its name is *mokat aku,* which means ghost conductor, carrier, bridge or step. *Aku* is the word used for the simple log rafts that carry people across the Baliem, or the pole that people walk to cross an irrigation ditch. The purpose of the *mokat aku* is to attract and then transport a ghost away from either a village or a garden. Its shape and design vary widely from place to place and builder to builder, but its basic features

[89]

usually include two upright sticks with a horizontal bar, much like a hurdle or carpenter's horse. A diagonal forms a letter N with the two uprights, one of which is a single pole with a nest or cradle on the upper end formed from the crotch of a branch. A dead rat or a piece of sugar cane is tied to the longitudinal cross-piece or put into the crotch of the upright. Both rat and sugar cane serve as a kind of bait to attract ghosts that might otherwise cause harm to plants or pigs, but they also have other significance. Like only one or two other plants, sugar cane must not be burned in a fire. To do so would be to risk sickness or some other trouble. Cane is also one of the most important ingredients of a ceremony called the *pelabi,* or "cutting away of mud," which is performed by close relatives six or eight weeks following a death.

Rats are used in a great variety of magical and ceremonial procedures. Often, especially when a man has been hit by an arrow in the stomach, a rat is caught and its belly opened with a bamboo knife. If the instrument cuts through the stomach wall or damages any other internal part, the outlook for the wounded man is not good, but if the opening simply displays the rat's viscera whole and healthy, the creature is hung up by the fire in the men's house as an augury signifying rapid recovery.

Whenever the Dani engage in tasks considered dangerous because of possible magical consequences—for example, handling corpses during funerals—they take pains to neutralize the charge generated by such contact. In many cases they need only be subjected to *sué palek,* or "removal by feather." When, for example, men have deposited a corpse for burning on the fire, one of them takes a small feather wand (often a red parrot feather stuck into the end of a short straw) and passes it slowly over the hands of those contaminated. The feather draws off the potential danger to which handling a corpse, building a watchtower, making shell ornaments and a series of other diverse activities makes one vulnerable.

In cases involving real sickness—say an infection caused by a cold or wound—the Dani employ a great variety of curative measures. Most common is for someone, preferably a *wesarun* (curer) to blow with rapid, shallow breaths on the infected spot. Aside from its curative effect, blowing also has a beneficial effect on the sick man's *etai-eken,* which are in need of every tonic available. Also, in the case of severe physical pain or discomfort, nettled plants will often be applied to an area free from pain so as to transfer the sensation of pain from one part to another.

Of great frequency is the sterner measure of letting blood. For the Dani, blood has immense significance. Its vital function is not appreciated with any scientific sophistication; yet it is known to contain at least part of the secret of life. The Dani know that life is dependent upon it, and they believe that in order to be healthy, blood must be pure, not corrupted or sick in the way a wound can make it. They also feel that all is well as long as the flesh is not torn or punctured, thereby exposing blood to a variety of contacts with the external world. However, it is assumed that the blood is immediately contaminated when one is wounded. It is said that the blood becomes dark, and this is considered bad. Nearly every wound, therefore, is treated by drawing off a quantity of "tainted" blood through incisions in the flesh around the wound, or by punctures made by shooting small arrows into the vein of an arm or leg.

Just as there are remedies built on superstitions, the etiology of most Dani ailments is equally imaginary. If a man breaks his leg by falling on a rocky path, it is perfectly apparent to him that his leg was broken by the fall. What he must supply for his own satisfaction is the *reason* for falling. In such a case the ghosts would certainly be blamed, at least indirectly. Occasionally there are reasons other than ghosts for certain special complaints. For example, a wenlike growth on the wrist has a known cause: it comes from chips of a particular flint that leap into the wrist when one works at gardening. In this malady the damage is caused by the flint itself; no further explanation of how it got into the wrist is sought. It may go or stay, and no very radical treatment is required.

Besides ghosts and inanimate objects there is a third reason for sickness, and that is human. People can do one another harm by either open violence or by secret magic. The Dani are not overly concerned with such matters, but they do attribute certain physical complaints to the malevolence of sorcerers and witches. There are at least two kinds of black magic. One is called *imak* and is practiced by women in a clan complex to the north; the other is called *guwarep* and is practiced by men who live in another group of clans to the south and east. It is striking that though deaths are attributed to some of these outsiders, there is no noticeable resentment against them. However, they are feared, perhaps largely because there is no reliable antidote, and people who are diagnosed as victims are given by others (and give themselves) little chance to recover. *Imak* magic is caused by mice, controlled by the sorcerer, which fasten vampire-fashion on the flesh of the victim's stomach. As a result the stomach swells and the man soon perishes.

Guwarep is a fine white powder which its practitioners can project into the sweet potatoes eaten by intended victims, causing a slow but certain death. Before she had died one woman was treated for such poisoning. Being ill, her *etai-eken* were shrunken and lifeless so that she had to be protected from ghosts as well. A tripod of stout poles was constructed near her home and she was put into it, carrying a bow and arrow; with these she would be able to defend herself from ghosts. Her small child was handed to her; since he was still an infant and had negligible *etai-eken,* he also was vulnerable to the ghosts. Placed on the tripod off the ground, the sick woman was told by her close relatives to cure herself, using the bow and arrow and the feather that was put into her hair as a symbol of health. But despite the ceremony, which included the killing of a medium-sized pig and the complete restoration of the small ghost house behind the men's house, the woman died about two months later. Perhaps her family and friends were right when they said she was the victim of an incurable disorder.

Though some Dani say that only humans have *etai-eken,* most believe that all creatures except the very lowest have them and therefore are subject to spells of both health and illness. This may be why part of Dani magic is devoted to looking after the second most important living beings, their pigs. In their cramped stall pigs are safe from the dangers of falling into an irrigation ditch and drowning, becoming lost or, most likely, being stolen. But they are never safe from the hungry mice and rats, which creep in at night to gnaw at their flesh. To prevent infection from a rat bite, the wound is treated with a combination of sticky pitch from the araucaria tree and a dusting of fine white ash. Pigs that have simply sickened, perhaps from the action of ghosts or sorcery, are sometimes smeared with the blood of another that has just been killed; this is thought to have exceptionally high curative and antidotal value. Otherwise such pigs may be fed sweet potatoes that have been magically smeared with such blood. Sometimes a mad woman from the north is asked to spit into the uncooked potatoes given her by the owners of the ailing pigs.

Perhaps because she is mad and because her madness is itself a sort of sickness which might be transmitted to the pigs, she hands the spit-treated sweet potatoes back with crossed arms—as if by returning them in this fashion the double negative of mad spit and twisted presentation will make a positive cure.

The chronicle of Dani magical practices, so many of which are designed to relieve real sickness or to combat imagined adversaries, is too long to recount in full. Probably it will never be done, since, with the advent of new illnesses and shifts in fortunes which characterize social life everywhere, the magic is a continuously changing phenomenon. Nonetheless, certain major ceremonies live on and are repeated with the same regularity as the realities they celebrate: birth, coming of age and death. To these, as well as the inevitable crisis of sickness, must be added the persistent danger of living in a world populated by ghosts. When a child is born it is given a name, a special relationship with a relative of its mother's family and a gift of shells. These are acts of human enablement. From this beginning will follow more names, more friends and more gifts of shells. With a fair degree of certainty such a child, whether male or female, will be initiated with songs and gifts into maturity, and with more songs and gifts and the same shells that crowned his birth into the unselect company of ghosts.

It might be expected that any society which values the killing of its enemies as highly as does the Dani would be obliged to view the experience of death in a rather special way. Killing an enemy inevitably brings death to oneself or one's friends. However, tradition, which cannot influence natural death, can and does influence unnatural death. The high value which the Dani place upon killing their enemies is meaningful only when the killing is accomplished by certain traditional—that is, predictable—means. All Dani, and therefore their enemies, know these traditions well. This does not mean that all Dani are prepared to die, or even that they are all equally equipped to avoid the fatal hazards by which they are continuously surrounded. What each must know about how he might be killed is subject to individual differences of temperament and mood. Warriors entering battles may do so with cunning, cowardice or false confidence. Women working in gardens near enemy territory may be alert or sleepy. Sometimes a woman going to work in such a garden never stops until she has reached the enemy, where she may be promptly killed or simply taken into the group. If she is killed, people say that she wanted to die rather than live with her husband or his other wives. Despite their incomplete grasp of rules, Dani children are probably most secure. Only if their trust in some adult who is meant to protect them has been misplaced is their life particularly endangered. But this is rare; otherwise the frequency of violent deaths for both children and adults would be far greater.

To be aware of *what* one's enemies are apt to do in order to kill is not necessarily to know *when*. As in all other matters, the Dani approaches problems of safety along the two paths of common sense and magic; that is, he attempts to insure his survival with a mixture of reason and faith. Reason dictates, for example, that a man be armed with his bow and arrow, spear or at least a heavy stick wherever he goes. Custom makes exceptions to this rule; when visiting a friendly village, a man will leave his weapons outside rather than create an air of belligerency. Also, men rarely go singly unless it be for a short distance and near their own village. Usually a companion or two is sought in the event of trouble, which can spring up with friendly as well as enemy neighbors.

On their way to the watchtowers in the morning, men are especially alert for any unusual footprints or trampled grass. They also pay close attention to the birds, for any absence from their customary thickets or groves may be a silent warning of intruders. Since it often rains at night in the Grand Valley, the paths and fields are usually cleared of the signs of the previous day's traffic, and fresh marks mean recent activity. When approaching danger areas, men walk quietly, never talking, because an enemy ambush must be heard the moment it is unleashed. The few seconds of silence may mean the difference between life and death—the chance to keep enough distance between yourself and your armed enemy.

During formal battles, which are fought on terrain each warrior has known since youth, safety depends on keeping a sure foot when skirmishing and in heeding the commands of elders and leaders. The man who has successfully avoided the hidden traps and open attacks of his enemy, as well as the hostility arising between allied people over stolen pigs or secluded women, is still alive more because of prudence and alertness than strength or bravery.

In Dani culture there is still another domain lying somewhere between reason and myth, and beyond magic, to which the Dani, like all other people, resort from time to time. They are religious for many reasons, but the principal one, as perhaps for most other people, is that they are sometimes afraid. Since they believe that humans linger after death, their religion is largely concerned with guiding and controlling the ghosts. Since the enemy also die and become ghosts, and since the Dani are a warrior society, it is not strange that the ghosts of both sides continue the hostilities they began in life. Ghosts are almost as real as anything alive, but because they are not alive in the same way as a mouse or a bird, the Dani relationship to them is not based on any

ordinary etiquette. The mere existence of ghosts necessitates a formal system of ceremonial and religious expressions; to influence them requires a great deal of work, the sacrifice of time, possessions and even parts of one's living self.

A Dani funeral is an awesome and remarkable occasion. Not all are alike, since a person's sex and the way in which death occurs determine many of the details. Nearly always, a male death is more important, though the natural death of an insignificant old man might cause less anguish than the unexpected death of an important woman. Deaths caused by illness, age or accident are less important than those resulting from enemy action. The death of a powerful leader, or *kain,* at the hands of the enemy is the most important of all. It is also the rarest, since *kains* are not apt to risk their lives unnecessarily—not only because they enjoy life but also because they do not want to provide the enemy with an opportunity for so much rejoicing.

A funeral is held the first full day following death. The corpse, lodged overnight in the long family house or sometimes in the round men's house, is propped against a wall with short lengths of banana tree trunk wedged under its knees, which are drawn up toward its chest. This is done in order to let the body stiffen in a sitting posture. If the funeral is for a person recently killed by the enemy (a "fresh-blood funeral"), soon after the sun rises a chair is made from sticks of *kai* wood, the same wood used to construct the watchtowers or *kaios.* This chair, or *pia,* is the only article of furniture made by the Dani. It has a seat about four feet from the ground, a back and two sides which rise to a little more than five feet. When the seat has been lined with a cushion of coarse grass, the corpse is brought from its resting place and is lifted into place. The corpse sits on the *pia* with knees bent nearly to its chin, its feet on the seat. A noose is made with bits of raffia to keep the head from lolling too far forward so that mourners are able to see the object of their grief.

Installed upon its temporary throne, the corpse is placed in the center of the courtyard facing the entrance of the compound. Most compounds are large enough so that in front and in back of the *pia,* the areas in which the women and the men congregate respectively, there are fifty or more feet of open ground to the nearest fence or building. To each side is less room, perhaps only ten or fifteen feet. Into the courtyard come the mourners. The first women move close to the *pia* as soon as the men who have lifted the corpse into it are satisfied that it is secure. The mourning chants the women sing do not cease until night has fallen and everyone who does not live in the funeral village has left. Those who stay will cry until the sun rises once again.

As a rule, a death is felt more deeply by women than by men. Both sexes give ample indication of their grief, but women, especially those most closely linked to the dead by kinship or marriage, seem driven by a deeper passion, whereas the men seem almost self-conscious. The funeral is arranged and carried out by men; they make the chair, slaughter the pigs, cook the feast, distribute the shell strings, construct the pyre and immolate the corpse. All ritual and other formalities are their responsibility, as is the task of killing an enemy in revenge.

Like all other Dani ceremonies, a funeral is an occasion for eating pigs. Depending on the importance of the person who has died, the number and size of pigs will vary, but the manner in which they are slaughtered, butchered, cooked and eaten is always the same. The pigs are supplied by individuals or by groups who have a particularly close connection with the deceased. A man who is especially rich and who has lost a particularly important relative might give more than one pig, together with shell bands, exchange stones and even feather goods. Some of these are redistributed the same day, while others are kept in honor of the dead person. Such largess is never wasted, however, because a man who gives lavishly knows that he will be repaid on future occasions when goods are exchanged again.

As soon as most of the gifts of shells and feather goods have been placed with the corpse on the *pia,* young men pick up the doomed pigs, one holding the ears, others holding the two hind legs. The animals are dispatched with bloodletting arrows shot into the heart from a distance seldom greater than a foot. Ears and tails are removed when the slaughtering is over and kept as tokens and reminders in the men's house. Fires are quickly lit to burn off the bristles, and experienced hands, using bamboo knives and stone axes, begin the butchering. In a short time the meat is divided into parts which will be either cooked immediately, saved for later feasting or retained for use in magic connected with the funeral. The jawbones are invariably removed and hung within the men's house. Like the ears and tails, they recall the occasion.

While the pigs are prepared for cooking, the steam pit is readied. Stones are heated and the pit is cleaned of refuse and relined with the long grass that will eventually envelop the contents— successive layers of meat, ferns, sweet potatoes and hot stones liberally sprinkled with water to produce steam. As the cooking is done, timed by long experience and all the chores that tradition regulates, men talk, women sing and death is conscientiously observed. The pit is opened when the food is judged ready and people begin to eat. A funeral is not primarily a feast, but no ceremony as important could occur without providing such valuables as sweet potatoes and pigs. It is more accurate to think of these as participants rather than as commodities. People partake with restraint at a funeral; little time is spent over the meal, for a great deal remains to be done.

After eating, several men who are close kin to the person who has died move over to the *pia*, and with a rising groan of objection from the women, remove the shell bands which have draped the corpse since early morning. The women are aware that the final rites are about to start, that in a matter of minutes the individual to whom they have given such close attention and who has been so palpably among them will be taken from their midst and put on the burning pyre. Now they witness the conspiring of their men as they deliberate the question of who shall receive which shell bands. These are laid neatly in rows on several banana leaves, and the most influential men of the community sit near them, whispering suggestions or canvassing opinions. One of the results of a Dani funeral is that wealth in the form of pigs, shell bands, nets and feather headbands is redistributed. Those who give are given back something else, or are promised a return at some future time, perhaps at the *mawe*, the great feast and exchange ceremony when many debts are paid and still more are contracted.

When the distribution of the shell bands is decided, a man, always important and always closely related to the person who has died, stands to call each recipient's name and hand him his new possession. This done, the corpse is untied and carried from the *pia* to the banana leaves on which the shell bands had been resting. Here the body is anointed with fat pressed from a piece of one of the slaughtered pigs. (All Dani cover themselves with pig fat whenever it is available. It is considered not only healthy but cosmetic to do so. A man feels elegant almost in proportion to the amount of fat applied to his hair, face and body; without any, he feels untidy and even a little mortified.) The corpse is greased in death as he would like to be in life, the only difference

being that this last time the fat is made holy by the ritual surrounding his death.

Now the rhythm of activity quickens and timing becomes more critical. While the corpse is anointed, the *pia* is dismantled and the wood for the pyre is arranged over the place where the corpse had sat all day. When the logs are arranged in a suitably high and steady platform, kindling underneath is lit from a brand. As the fire gains headway, the corpse is lifted in the arms of its closest kinsmen and put on the smoking pyre. At the same time two other men arise, one to hold a meager bundle of grass above the body, the other standing near to shoot into it an arrow which will release the spirit of the man just committed to the fire when it strikes the bundle. The bundle and its intruding arrow are then carried to the compound entrance so that the ghost may depart with ease.

Next, the spirit-forsaken corpse is covered with planks and logs which will insure its total incineration. The women watch, the volume of their mourning increasing until the flames engulf and consume the body. At last, like a settling storm, the wind of their despair subsides. The mood changes in their seated ranks, and they move to leave now that the ceremony is over. For three or sometimes four more days they will return, bringing netfuls of potatoes to share with other women and with their children. Some of the young girls will have a finger amputated; the boys will run through the village at the end of each day throwing stones ahead of them to chase ghosts out the entrance and down the path toward the frontier.

After the day of the cremation only the regular inhabitants of the compound participate in the extended funeral activities. They will help the women make the steam pit and eat the potatoes that come out of it. Slowly the warriors go back to their watchtowers, or to formal battles wherever they are announced. For them the best thing is to kill an enemy as quickly as possible.

One man, a specialist of sorts, has further funeral duties. He is the surgeon-magician whose appointment with the little girls chosen to sacrifice a finger falls at dawn on the morning following the cremation. The girls come into the family house with their mothers and a few older male relatives. The finger to be lost is tied between the second and third joint, and the child's elbow is rapped with a hard stick to deaden the nerves in part of her hand. With a small transverse stone adze, like that with which a woman might sharpen her digging stick, the amputator takes off the finger, extended on a board, up to the second joint. The severed member is burned in the dying embers of the funeral fire, and the wound is dressed with a mixture of clay and ashes. The child may cry or not, depending on its age and temperament. Each knows that what has happened had to happen, and that it will happen again. When they were infants their own mothers had held them and played with them using hands that were mostly thumbs.

Immediately after the amputation, the girl's hand is bound tightly with banana leaves and banana husk strings all the way to the elbow. With a palmful of grass beneath the bandaged elbow to catch the blood, the child will hold up her proud green fist for the rest of the day.

On the same morning, many nets brought by the throngs of women the day before are distributed to a smaller multitude of eligible recipients. The distribution of these awards is decided by the most important women, but the atmosphere of this exchange differs markedly from that of the men. The women are more openly conniving, and shout and argue loudly their opinions and feelings. The men never interfere.

The death of a Dani, especially if it has been caused by the enemy, changes the outlook of everyone allied to the losing side. The change is best expressed as a weakening or shrinking of their *etai-eken,* their seeds of singing. These seeds are continually active in the life-making process of every man or woman, and respond favorably or unfavorably to the events of each individual's career and destiny. They are not merely personal, however, though a person's seeds may have more influence on his development than on someone else's. For example, a death that is felt keenly by many people will have a bad effect on the *etai-eken* of a large portion of the group. The women feel bereft and deprived, the men disgraced and enfeebled. The Dani regard the killing of a comrade, wife or child personally as a physical and spiritual threat and as a spur to actions which will redress the unequal balance between themselves and the enemy. The sense of grief that all Dani experience when abandoned by someone close does not give way to mere revenge or self-pity. The need to reequalize the balance is only a partial cure, and it is a long time before anyone's death is forgotten, either privately or ritually, even when an enemy is killed and a victory has been celebrated.

5 Ghosts

p. 103 : **179.** A feather wand removes the **wusa,** or magic power, which clings to a man's hands after he has handled a corpse, woven a shell band or performed a ceremony. **Wusa** is not in itself good or bad, but if misused it can be dangerous. Thus, when moving from a sacred, **wusa**-charged activity to a profane one, a person must be desacralized.

p. 104 : **180.** The bird of the Dani immortality myth is the small black and white robin chat. In the myth the bird and the snake have an argument or run a race. Snake says that after men die and are cremated, they should come to life again; Bird says no, when men die they should stay dead. Bird wins, and so men are doomed to mortality. But Bird feels sorry for men, and smears its shoulders with white mud as a sign of mourning.

p. 104 : **181.** Two men make a small enclosure for ghosts in the banana grove behind a men's house. This is a magical lure to divert the ghosts from living people.

p. 104 : **182.** A girl jokingly imitates a ghost. Even though the Dani are constantly surrounded by malevolent ghosts, and most of their ritual is directed toward placating ghosts, the people are not particularly fearful or pious in their feelings about them.

p. 104 : **183.** A magic bow and arrows are made as symbolic weapons to be placed within the watchtower so that ghosts can help the men defend against an enemy attack.

p. 105 : **184.** Weapons and ornaments from enemy dead are displayed at the **etai** dance. These trophies are called "dead men" or "dead birds," for the Dani recognize a symbolic relationship between man and bird. The bundle of trophies is kept hidden in a special house, and is brought out and set up at one end of the dance ground where the older men sit.

p. 106 : **185.** Sacred stones are taken out of a special cabinet in the men's house for renewal and consecration during a ceremony held every year or so. These stones are the most sacred Dani object, and each one is the personal property of a man and his sons. Several closely related men or intimate friends may keep their stones together.

p. 106 : **186.** On the path to the brine pool lies an eroded limestone rock which is said to be a woman turned to stone by an angry ghost.

p. 106 : **187.** The sun's house is in a narrow valley running east to the Grand Valley. The Dani say that the sun is a woman dressed like a warrior. She leaves her house in the morning to travel across the sky. At the end of the day she sits down on a mat and travels back through the sky to her house in the east, where she spends the night. The stilts and bark roof of the sun's house are unique features found in no other Grand Valley Dani houses.

p. 106 : **188.** Valuable exchange stones, decorated with furs and feathers, are laid out on folded nets during certain parts of the funeral ceremony. The stones and nets are assembled by close relatives of the dead person, and they are displayed to placate his ghost by demonstrating the concern of the living for the dead.

p. 107 : **189.** To help protect a wounded man from ghosts, the people of his compound prepare a bundle of special plants and a feathered wand.

p. 107 : **190.** To make the wand, various kinds of feathers are put in the tips of a reedy branch.

p. 107 : **191.** Shouting at the ghosts who may be lurking about the compound to take advantage of the weakened condition of the wounded man, two boys run with the feathered wands to the paths leading to the compound. There they plant the wands as warnings to the ghosts.

p. 108 : **192.** His head draped in a woman's carrying net, a recently wounded man knits a cowrie shell band. Between his teeth he holds a bone awl. When a person is wounded or sick or in mourning, his **etai-eken** are particularly vulnerable to ghostly attacks; hence, to escape the ghosts' notice, he camouflages his presence with a net cowl.

p. 109 : **193–201.** The Dani employ a multitude of barriers of branches, reeds and grasses to protect their gardens and compounds from the malevolence of ghosts.

Preparing the Funeral Meal

p. 110 : **202–210.** The pigs which have been brought by the funeral guests are killed with bows and arrows (202). The slaughtered pigs are arranged in front of the men's house, and shouted over so that the ghosts will take notice and be placated. Then ears and tails are cut off (203). The ears will be roasted and eaten; the tails

will become magical neck ornaments. The pigs are butchered with bamboo knives and stone adzes (204, 205, 206). The cooking pit for the steam bundle is cleaned out (207) and lined with grass (208). Stones, heated in a large fire, are carried to the cooking pit, where they are deposited in alternating layers with vegetables, pork and grasses (209). When the steam bundle is complete, it is covered with grass, lashed with stout vines and allowed to cook for about an hour (210).

p. 111 : **211, 212.** Men make up separate packages of pork wrapped in banana leaf for the steam bundle.

p. 111 : **213.** When the pigskins are cooked with their thick layer of fat, men cut them into small pieces with a bamboo knife. Each guest receives a piece; he smears part on his skin and then eats the rest.

p. 111 : **214.** The steam bundle is carefully constructed in alternating layers of food, leaves and hot rocks.

pp. 112–113 : **215.** When the steam bundle has cooked for an hour or so, the women dismantle it and the food is distributed to the funeral guests.

p. 114 : **216.** The corpse in its funeral chair (or **pia**) is surrounded by mourners. Nets, headdresses, cowrie shell bands and other valuables are draped on the chair and the body itself.

p. 115 : **217–225.** The funeral chair is constructed in the courtyard of the compound where a person has just died of battle wounds. Cremation takes place in the mid-afternoon of the day after the death, the first day of the funeral ceremony. If the person has died of sickness or old age, the corpse is simply kept in the family house until the funeral pyre is lit, but if it is a "fresh-blood death," caused by battle, it is displayed in a chair in the courtyard of the victim's compound. The body is lashed into the chair and slowly covered with valuables brought by the funeral guests.

p. 116 : **226, 227.** Cowrie shell bands that were brought to the funeral and draped around the corpse are removed just before the cremation, laid on the ground and then carefully distributed. In theory, relatives of the dead person's mother bring shell goods, relatives of the dead person's father bring pigs, and an exchange is then made. In fact, these categories are not rigidly observed. Both the bringing and the taking of funeral gifts is accompanied by shouting that informs the ghost of the deceased that the living are concerned about it.

p. 116 : **228, 229.** Women's carrying nets, brought as gifts during the first day of the funeral, are redistributed by women during the second day.

p. 117 : **230–234.** The cremation itself (230) takes place in the midafternoon, after the communal eating of pig and sweet potatoes, and after the shell bands have been given out. Young men bring in heavy wood for the pyre (231); the corpse is smeared with pig grease by the closest relatives (232). As it is carried to the burning pyre (233), the mourning voices reach a crescendo; then, as the corpse is being covered with more wood, a man shoots an arrow into a grass bundle (234). This is quickly carried to the compound entrance, to help the ghost on its way out of the body and away from the survivors.

pp. 118–119 : **235.** As the funeral pyre consumes a boy's body, his mother writhes in lonely mourning.

The Attitudes of Mourning

p. 120 : **236–244.** A mother cries alone as her child's corpse is laid on the pyre (236, 237, 238, 239); a man rubs his thigh (240), and a woman holds her hand to her head (241). Sitting women clasp the funeral chair (242, 243); an important man sings a dirge (244).

p. 121 : **245–247.** A woman newly arrived at a funeral stands to mourn (245); seated women cry and moan (246, 247).

pp. 122–123 : **248.** From a crowd of mourning women, one waves helplessly toward the corpse.

p. 124 : **249.** As the funeral pyre burns down in the dusk, many of the guests depart.

p. 124 : **250.** The morning after the cremation, a woman of the compound picks remnant bones from the dead coals. They will be wrapped in a banana leaf and hung in the family house for a few days.

p. 124 : **251.** When the first part of the funeral is over, the burned bones are deposited in a small enclosure, the "bone fence," behind the men's house.

p. 124 : **252.** Deep in the forest, every clan has a small structure which holds memorial bundles, one for each member who has died.

p. 125 : **253.** These young girls with bandaged hands have just lost one or two fingers early on the second day of the funeral ceremony. After the hand has been numbed by a blow on the elbow, the fingers are chopped off with a blow from a stone adze. Like pigs and shell goods, the fingers are gifts considered necessary to placate the ghosts. Although nearly every Dani girl loses several fingers, as a woman she does a wide range of work, from gardening to making nets, with great manual skill.

p. 126 : **254–256.** Small rodents assume unaccustomed importance on one day of the long funeral ceremony. Men and boys spend the morning searching through grassy fields and fallow gardens for the small creatures, which are then brought back to the funeral and cleaned, roasted and eaten.

p. 126 : **257.** The symbolic feast of roast pork, sugar cane and sweet potatoes takes place during the second phase of the funeral, some six weeks after cremation. Like other parts of the ceremony, this ritual is supposed to placate the ghost. A close relative of the dead person takes a bite of the three foods, chews, and then spits it out, while an old man shouts to the ghost "You eat! You eat!"

p. 127 : **258.** Decorating himself with spots of mud, a boy prepares for the **etai,** or victory dance.

p. 127 : **259–261.** Women smear themselves with mud for the victory dance.

pp. 128–134 : **262–280.** The **etai** is celebrated for two days after the killing of an enemy. People come from the entire alliance area, dressed in their finest furs, feathers and shells and smeared with pig grease and colored mud, to dance and sing. This is a ritual calling the attenion of the ghosts to the killing and saying in effect, "Look what we have done for you! Now leave us alone." Singing and shouting, men and boys run in great circles. From noon until dark they dance for two days. It is a celebration less of the death of an enemy than of the knowledge that the malevolent ghosts are placated for the moment.

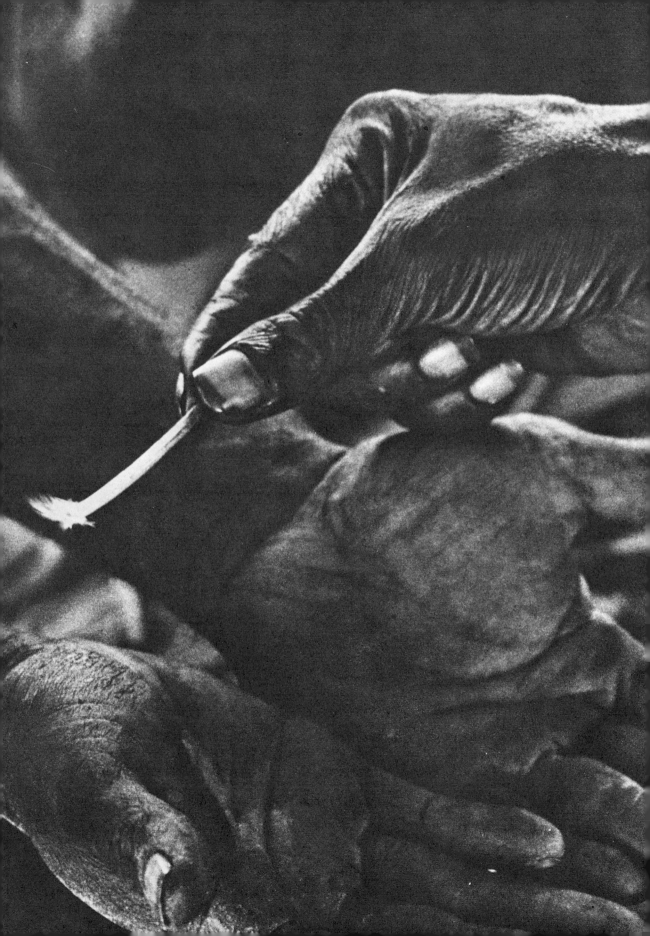

180

181

182

183

185

186

187

188

189

190

191

193   194   195

196   197   198

199   200   201

202

203

208

207

211

212

213

220

221

217

218

219

222

223

224

225

226

227

228

229

230

231

232

233

234

236

237

238

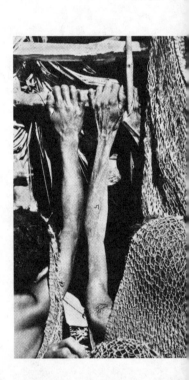

240

241

243

[120]

246

249

250

251

25

254

255

256

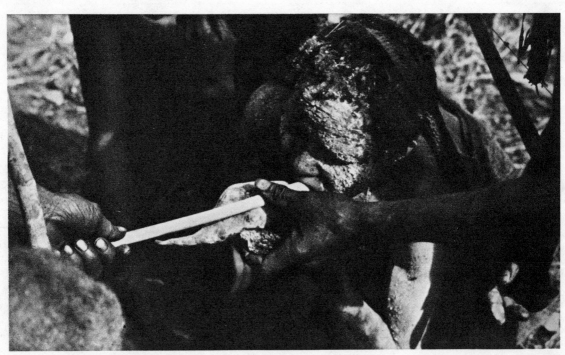

257

258

259

260

261

264

265

266

267

268

269

270

271

272

[129]

275

276

277

278

6 Violence

The Dani word *weem* means two things: a kind of knife made of splinters of bamboo and (for lack of a better English equivalent) war. It is difficult to call a Dani *weem* a war since it involves almost none of the things that this has come to mean in the civilized world. True, *weem* is organized fighting between political groups, but it springs from very different motives and anticipates very different results. In the first place, it is as positively sanctioned as any major institution in the culture. The Dani fight because they want to and because it is necessary. They do not enter into battle in order to put an end to fighting. They do not envisage the end of fighting any more than the end of gardening or of ghosts. Nor do they fight in order to annex land or to dominate people. The Dani are warriors because they have wanted to be since boyhood, not because they are persuaded by political arguments or their own sentimental or patriotic feelings. They are ready to fight whenever their leaders decide to do so.

Such decisions are the responsibility of a small number of *kains,* or influential men, living in the territory of Kosi-Alua, the Willihiman-Wallalua, or other confederations that together make up the Kurelu alliance. Each of these men has influence in one of the clan and village groups which together form an alliance of fighting men spread across an area of approximately thirty-five square miles. Adjacent to this territory live other confederations, speaking the same language and sharing the same culture, but comprising an enemy alliance. The fifty thousand or more Dani of the Grand Valley are divided into some dozen alliances, each a potential enemy of the others.

The opposing alliances are separated by a frontier guarded on both sides of a no man's land by watchtowers, and lookouts man these from dawn till dark. Their task is entirely defensive, unless they spot an enemy raid. Then they give the alarm, and unless hopelessly out-numbered, will engage the raiding group. Watchtowers are

[135]

seldom more than a few minutes' run apart, and though there may be as few as two or three men close to the watchtower itself, many others will be working in nearby gardens with their weapons never more than a few paces from them. Thus, with a few shouts, a defense or even a strategic counteroffense can be organized in a matter of moments.

Behind the emergencies and alarms, the attacks and counterattacks, which demand only a small part of the time and energy devoted to the institution of war, lies a complex and far-reaching system of beliefs and behavior. In the first place, the Dani engage in "war" to promote the success and well-being of their social order. In large measure, their health, welfare and happiness depend on the pursuit of aggression against their traditional enemies. Since their enemies share a common culture, the same considerations motivate them. For both, the various forms that aggression takes are their means to secure, even if only temporarily, a sort of harmony between their desires for personal safety and certain inescapable pressures that militate against such desires.

The greatest of these pressures is exerted by the ghosts, but there are other influences, such as the goading of women who want their men to revenge the death of a husband, son or brother. The major inducement, however, is the Dani's sense of obligation to the ghosts. It is assumed that until the ghosts are avenged the people themselves will suffer. The ghosts may trouble them with accidents, sickness, blights upon their crops, droughts, floods or any of a multitude of other distresses. For Dani warriors the risks involved in fighting an occasional battle, or even joining the far more dangerous occasional raiding parties, which are a more promising way to kill an enemy, are not nearly as great as those to be encountered were they to ignore the demands of unavenged ghosts.

It must also be remembered that all Dani men are professional fighters. They have been trained since learning how to walk in all the techniques of war. Of course there is a difference in ability between individual warriors, but all except the totally incapacitated are expertly schooled. Many of the finest warriors, in fact, are blind in one eye or have a deformed limb, and they compensate with superior cunning for defects that would be more serious handicaps in open and indiscriminate warfare.

Being equal to the task of fighting, the Dani do not regard the hazards involved with the apprehension felt by amateur or part-time soldiers. Each warrior knows not only the extent of danger involved, but is aware of his own ability; hence he can participate with considerable confidence of surviving. What cannot be calculated is the accidental and the unexpected, and it is this that is responsible for the occasional death.

Dani fighting can be divided into two basic categories: formal battles and raids. A battle may be instigated by one's own group or by the enemy. The privilege of calling a battle (which is literally what happens) is the prerogative of a very small group of important war leaders. When the decision has been made by one of these leaders, a band of his men will go early in the morning to the frontier and challenge the enemy by shouting across no man's land. Almost invariably the challenge is accepted by a leader on the other side, and both groups begin to spread the news to their neighbors. The cries can often be heard as the sun begins to throw long, pointed shadows from the eastern ridge across the valley floor, and the information passes in ever-diminishing waves of sound traveling north and south to the remotest villages. Mixed with the words that announce the place for gathering is the mimicked song of the *yoroick,* a rufous dove that inhabits the forests interspersed among the villages. This

[136]

sound is jubilant and expectant; it anticipates the tumult that characterizes all Dani battles. In half an hour the word will have spread to all concerned, and for the following couple of hours the men of the various villages will decide whether to fight that day. Most will prefer immediate battle. Only those of the villages most distant from the appointed battlefield may decide that it is too far to go, or that the day looks as if it held rain. The recently wounded will also stay at home, since the Dani believe that a wounded man's impaired *etai-eken* are particularly vulnerable to the malevolence of ghosts. It is for this reason that the wounded drape their heads, cowl fashion, with a small carrying net. They hope that it will disguise them and prevent their recognition by the ghosts.

From about eight until ten o'clock the men who will fight that day eat their morning meal of sweet potatoes and prepare for battle. It is a casual time except for those living at a great distance who must spend the time journeying to the battleground (*weem holak:* literally, war trail). If rain does not put an end to the fighting, most warriors will spend the next six or seven hours without food, and so they are careful to eat well while it is still possible to do so. This is also the time when the men are concerned with their appearance; a formal battle is one of the few occasions when they want to look their best. Everyone who has any—or who can borrow some from a friend—rubs pig fat on his body. Some will take out their war headdresses, the fronts of which are bedecked with the rare bird-of-paradise plumes that sway to their owner's movements. Everyone will wear what he has or can borrow to enhance his appearance. Some will carry whisks made of feathers of the cassowary bird; others will take long, slender wands of pure white egret feathers. Some will wear pig tusks in their noses, others circlets of egret or

parrot feathers on their heads. Some will daub their legs or shoulders with gray, orange or red clay so as to resemble their ideal of birds. In battle, or perched on a rock waiting for action, the plumed and painted Dani warrior looks as if he might indeed take flight.

By the forenoon—usually no later than eleven o'clock—bands of warriors are on their way to the appointed battleground or are already sitting in clusters of fighting groups under the shelter of a watchtower close by. Many of these will remain at such a rendezvous even when the skirmishing has begun. They act as a reserve, held back to protect the frontier from a surprise attack and also to give support to the front if it is needed.

As with so many other points of procedure during a battle, it is understood that fighting will not start until both sides are ready. During the movement of warriors toward the front, the leaders, especially the men who have called the battle, make final preparations for the day. They discuss alternative strategies and conduct a variety of magical ceremonies. Neither the strategy nor the magic is ever the same for each battle, just as the cure for what might appear to be the same ailment differs for each individual.

Generally speaking, the magic before a battle is mainly divinatory. That is, the leaders who have committed themselves to a battle are primarily interested in knowing the outcome, and they wish to consult all possible signs for evidence of what the immediate future holds. For this reason, around the area occupied by the battle leaders, men too young and too old to fight look for small living creatures such as grasshoppers, birds and small rodents. These are bound up with grass and presented to the leaders, who are gratified and encouraged because the creatures symbolize dead enemy warriors. Or the battle leader may pass among his followers a small pig as a particularly potent talisman insuring success.

At other times the older men who are not fighting will trace in the ashes of the fire a path pointing in the direction of the battleground after their younger comrades have gone forward from their intermediate position short of the battleground itself. This path enables the ghosts to see where the fighting will take place and encourages them to join the warriors.

By noon, most of the warriors have arrived and the various formations have taken more or less final positions. Some are armed with bows and arrows, some with spears. The opposing armies are deployed so that between the most forward elements of each there lies a battle-ground of perhaps five hundred yards. A mood of silent but excited expectation pervades all ranks. From this point on, the day will bring the pleasures of the fight to several hundred on both sides, momentary terror for the handful who will feel the sudden pain of an enemy arrow, and, rarely, the unmentionable shock of death to someone who acts stupidly or clumsily.

The warriors in the forward and middle positions watch their enemy with mounting alertness. Each side waits for the characteristic opening to such battles—the advance of a party of perhaps thirty or forty who come forward to reconnoiter the open terrain and to test their enemies' attitude. This is called *weem iya,* a sort of ceremonial thrust in the direction of the enemy. As a rule, a similar party of the enemy, usually the band of men who form the temporary front line, respond to this gesture by advancing in cautious stages: running, then stopping, then running forward several more paces. When the two groups are fifty yards apart, bowmen are likely to loose one or two arrows at their opposite numbers, more as a gesture of readiness to engage than in a serious attempt to do harm. After a few minutes, both groups will turn and fall back in the direction of their main forces. At a shorter distance from the enemy than before, they will stop and wait until the time has come to make another sally toward the front. This preliminary fencing is almost entirely ritual, like that of Japanese wrestlers, who confront each other with characteristic squats and bows before the sudden furious struggle begins.

After three or even more such sallies by the forward groups, and at a moment determined by a multitude of obvious and obscure cues, the symbolic release of arrows gives way to deadly fighting. As the front erupts with motion—no longer the stylized ballet of the previous half hour but an unchoreographed but still graceful cavorting of men dodging the haphazard flight of spears and arrows—a mass of warriors rises from the middle ground of both camps and runs, bunched and ready, to the rhythmic sound of several hundred feet on the hard ground, toward the front and into action. Sustained fighting along an active and open front seldom lasts longer than ten or fifteen minutes and rarely involves more than two hundred men on each side—and usually less than half this number.

Each battleground offers different fighting conditions, and where on one day the maneuvering may be the skirmishing and disengagement just described, another battle may unfold in quite a different manner. For example, the leaders in charge may decide to employ one of the tactical moves that are basic elements in the art of Dani war to add what little element of surprise is possible in a contest with which all participants are fully familiar. Lacking such tactical resources a Dani battle would be an even safer undertaking than it is; with them, both sides can at least hope that their enemy may blunder into one of the simple traps each sets for the other. Each group knows all the possible traps and is well prepared against them, but in rare instances one may score with horrible unexpectedness.

The Dani have names for several such maneuvers. All are ambushes of one kind or another, but differ in the manner in which they are sprung. *Weem ape palek,* also called *weem talharek,* is an ambush from two sides. It succeeds only when there is sufficient time and cover to take positions without being seen and a sufficiently adroit front line to coax the enemy into the trap. Visually there is not enough cover to conceal an ambush, nor enough time or vegetation to reach such a position. Because all warriors fear an ambush more than anything else, they exercise the utmost caution when advancing toward the enemy, particularly if the surrounding terrain includes high grass or what may seem to be innocent scrub.

If the ambush is from one side only, it is called *weem lapularek.* Rarely does it or any variant succeed. Often an ambush is set, but almost always it is detected. Even if it is not, the enemy's front line is too wary of the possibility to ever come close enough to be attacked, and they are always careful to maintain an open route for retreat, called *lo pilili* (going quickly).

During the quarter hour or so of fighting along the active front fresh groups will frequently be sent in to join or replace those who have been bearing the brunt of the attack. When fifty or more men are shooting arrows, often no further away than fifty feet, their potential victims are obliged to stay continuously in motion, and this is exhausting as well as exhilarating work which requires incredible agility and concentration. Every warrior looks out for his companions as well as for himself, calling attention to arrows in flight or shooting rapidly to cover the retreat of a man who has flung his spear and thereby disarmed himself. Only in the closest and thickest fighting does a warrior risk his finest spear. Besides their best weapon, spearmen usually carry a shorter and less deadly "throw-away" one. A large spear is a valuable possession since the wood must be procured from the Yalis, who find it in their eastern forests, and it is an object prized by its owner and by the enemy. Along with certain other possessions, such as any shell ornaments, a feather whisk, headdress or human hair itself, a man's spear is, in the language of his enemy, an *ap warek,* a dead man. Other fighting groups in the Baliem call these trophies *sué warek,* or dead birds. Both refer to the measure of success in fighting—a success that at the very least means the capture of valuable belongings, and at best the killing of an enemy warrior who is stripped of his possessions.

The only time that a warrior does not look at what his enemy is doing is when he has turned to run back toward his own middle ground. It is partly for this reason that so many men are wounded by arrows in the back or buttocks. Though fired with respectable velocity, the arrows do not fly true, since none are feathered. This is surprising in light of the emphasis in Dani culture on birds, feathers and flight. A possible explanation may be that the Dani realize that if their arrows were feathered, many more warriors would be hit. Perhaps they know that even so small a change in the rules of war could disturb the delicate balance they have achieved between chance and competence, between the competing needs of life and death.

As the early afternoon wears on, the pace of battle develops into a steady series of brief clashes and relatively long interruptions. On a particularly clear day the bright highland sun may discourage the warriors, who exert themselves less willingly in the heat. Every foray of any size or intensity will provide some wounded on both sides. An arrow in one's limbs or scalp is not uncommon, since a man in the thick of battle tends to hide as much as possible behind his head, retracting his extremities and bending forward in the direction of his enemies. In cases where the wound is superficial, the victim gets out of range as quickly as possible. Dani arrows are made so that when they strike a person, particularly if he is in motion, a deliberately weakened portion of the foreshaft breaks off and leaves only the often intricately barbed tip embedded in the flesh. As soon as he has reached a safe distance from the front, a man so wounded will be taken by his friends to the shade of a tree, and there they will work the arrow out if it has not broken off deep inside. As soon as the offending tip is cut out, it is given to the wounded man, who keeps it to put with similar trophies in the rafters of his men's house. Usually the wound is bathed and then bandaged with leaves and grass strings. This will keep dirt and flies from entering the wound, but it will not halt the infection that often follows from the irritation caused by the bits of orchid fiber with which nearly all arrow tips are wound. This fiber often causes minor wounds to become progressively more serious. In fact, half the deaths in all Dani fighting can be attributed to infection.

When a man has been hit in the belly, back or chest, both his own shock and the concern of his companions are evident. As soon as possible he is lifted on the shoulders of a kinsman or fellow villager and carried gently to shade well back of the battle area. There he is put down and made as comfortable as possible against a tree, or is propped up in the arms of a friend. By word of mouth the nature of his wound immediately becomes known to his companions, and if the skill of a specialist in arrow removal is required, he will be sent for quickly. Such a specialist does not restrict his activities to surgery, so he may have to be sought at the battlefront itself.

Since Dani arrows are often barbed, their removal can be delicate and painful. Still, it is not for these reasons that the specialist is called; almost anyone with good eyes and steady hands can work the arrow free. The specialist is required for the surgery that custom prescribes in all serious wounds. The Dani believe that whenever blood is spilled, especially within one's body, it becomes the source of much pain and perhaps grave sickness. It is called *mep mili,* or dark blood, and their practice is to draw it off to prevent harm. The technique is both simple and painful. As soon as the arrow has been removed, the patient is held in an upright position so that the surgeon can make a series of incisions in his stomach wall. The specialist makes a horizontal fold of skin by pinching with one hand and cutting through it with a bamboo knife held in the other. Next, the knife point is inserted and punched inward about an inch, then turned upward so that it points toward the rib cage, where it is pushed inward another two or three inches. Usually a number of such punctures are made: several at the sides, and one approximately in the middle, higher on the body close to the solar plexus.

This last incision is the same as the others in that it is meant to channel off the *mep mili* resulting from the original arrow wound, but different in being made close to the site of the *etai-eken,* or soul matter. Besides taking the precaution of removing any dark blood that may have found its way into the *etai-eken* area, this is done to coax the *etai-eken* themselves back where they belong. When a man is seriously wounded, his relatives and friends imagine that the greatest potential danger lies in the possibility of the *etai-eken* being dislodged. To return them to their proper place may require the efforts and skills of more than one man. The specialist who has made the punctures may not be the person to recall the *etai-eken.* Whoever is designated or volunteers—as is usually the case—speaks to the *etai-eken* by blowing and murmuring in the victim's ear. He calls to them to return to their proper place and points to it with a small wand of tied grass called *aiginam,* which he holds against the forsaken solar plexus.

It is difficult to say how much the distress of a man who is wounded badly enough to be operated on is due to physical pain or to spiritual anguish. The tolerance for pain among these people seems very high. Neither a boy nor a man will ever cry out while undergoing surgery for the removal of an arrow, but often, especially after treatment for dark blood, their spirits sag and they are enveloped in what appears to be a combination of shock and gloom. No doubt they worry more about the condition and whereabouts of their *etai-eken* than about the blood they have lost or the infection they are risking. In any case, even if they are physically capable of walking, the badly wounded submit torpidly to being transported by their comrades in a stretcher, which is made from materials directly at hand. Its most important function, aside from bearing the weight of the wounded man, is to keep him hidden from the ghosts, and for this reason the body is swathed in grass. Four men think nothing of carrying another in the gathering darkness along slippery paths and across deep swamps for five or even ten miles. Behind them will be two or three other men carrying all the weapons.

An average day's fighting will consist of ten to twenty clashes between the opposing forces. By late afternoon, when the sun is nearing the top of the western valley wall, the men who have come the furthest will already be leaving, since they want to arrive home before night has completely fallen. If there is no time for another foray, the rest may prefer to sit on their side of the battle line and abuse their foes with taunts and epithets. Such tirades, hurled across two hundred yards of battleground, are almost as great a pleasure as the clash of arms, and they offer the opponents both release and vast amusement. Most warriors on either side know each other by name, and a surprising amount of their private lives is also common knowledge. Therefore the insults are often personal and will elicit laughter from both camps.

Gradually both sides withdraw, until by the time the sun has dropped behind the western ranges, only a handful of conscientious and wary young warriors remain to guard against the unlikely possibility of a surprise attack. In the twilight they then will break and run for home, racing the night and the ghosts they cannot see in the dark.

Aside from the formal battles, Dani warfare is marked by raids and other sorts of concealed attacks. While the battle is a highly stylized, almost social event conducted according to protocol and governed by conventions amounting almost to rules and regulations, the raid is a naked attempt to take a life by trick, deception or stratagem. In point of fact, because of the limitations of a restricted arsenal and because both sides are equally familiar with the terrain which must be crossed, the raid also has a certain patterned quality. One great difference between battles and raids is the matter of surprise: it is never known when the enemy will try to sneak through one's defenses and kill, whereas the whole countryside is aware of an impending battle. It is largely on account of the raids that Dani life is organized as it is. It accounts for the necessity of a no man's land, of watchtowers, of men spending much of their time on guard duty and making weapons, of keeping the grass short wherever the enemy might try to set up an ambush, of maintaining artificial ponds where ducks will rise if some one approaches, and of an elaborate set of magical practices that safeguard the system of defenses and warriors who man it. In short, raids form a significant portion of the total culture of the Dani people.

A raid is a desperate attempt to take an enemy life and has none of the theatricality of a formal battle. In the first place, it is restricted to certain trusted and eager warriors, usually those between twenty and thirty-five years old. The raiding party will often include men who are noted for their aggressiveness both in and out of battle, and usually some will be what the Dani call *hunukpalin*—men "cut off" from others by their apparent fearlessness. Though he will not actually participate in the conclusive stages of a raid, a leader of the first rank is always behind its organization to lend it the required sanction politically, magically and tactically. The raiding party itself will number between ten and twenty. Often they will choose a day that is overcast, or even bleak, misty and chill. On such days they can hope to find a few of the more diligent farmers who have come to work their gardens despite the discomforts of the weather, and they are less likely to run headlong into large parties of alert defenders.

As a rule, and in spite of the necessity for their remaining concealed, the members of a raiding party will spend the early morning dressing each other's hair, readying their weapons and preparing their ornaments. By the time they set forth toward the enemy garden area selected for attack, everyone in their own villages knows about the raid. Even though they have gone into their own gardens to work, other warriors who are not in the raiding party will bring their fighting paraphernalia with them.

The strategy of a raid follows a set procedure. First the party leaves by circuitous and hidden paths to meet at an assigned place near the frontier where they can be sure of not being seen and from which they can proceed stealthily through no man's land. Simultaneously there is a slow build-up of reserve forces at stations well back of the frontier. These too seek to attract no attention, for if they detected the forces, enemy lookouts would know that something was afoot. Then the raiding party penetrates into enemy territory, where they will either remain in ambush or attack, depending on what targets present themselves. The move forward by the various supporting forces gives cover to the raiding party that will be exposed once it has gone into action. Finally, the raiding party withdraws after its attempted ambush or attack, and the quickly mobilized enemy is engaged in battle by the reserve forces.

Of course, this is only a sketchy outline of how things may go. A raid depends on so many uncontrollable and variable factors that chance often plays a greater role than planning. For instance, the whole outcome of such an expedition depends on whether or not the raiders are seen—a fact they will not necessarily ascertain until the enemy decides to stage its own ambush and trap the unwary invaders. Second, much depends on whether a farmer has come along to work his field, or whether a small enough group of enemy warriors can be surprised at a relatively isolated watchtower. Moreover, it is crucial that the raiders attack swiftly and accurately so that the instantaneous alarm does not arouse the enemy in sufficient numbers to counterattack or to cut off the invaders' line of retreat. Lastly, the supporting forces must keep in close enough touch with the raiding party to know where they are at all times and to be in a position to render aid without giving themselves and the existence of the raid itself away. For all these reasons, raiding is an extremely dangerous activity for both quarry and hunter.

One day, after some weeks of waiting through several formal battles for an opportunity to avenge the death of Weake, a small boy stabbed to death by the Wittaia during a recent ambush, the Willihiman-Wallalua were ready to stage their own raid. The expedition was organized by Wereklué, one of the few men who could take responsibility for an act of war. The participants, a band of determined relatives of Weaké, included Tegé Warek, Tekman Biok, Aloro, Umue, Siba, Huonké, Apeori, Asukpalek, Agukweak, Hanomoak, Oatlabu, Pilaké, Husak and Yonokma. Wereklué had decided that the raid should be directed at a Wittaia garden lying to the southwest of the Watibara. The members of the raiding party got off to an early start under a low cloud cover which hung heavily just above the treetops. The warriors followed the valley of the Aikhé, keeping away from open ground and trailing their long spears behind them. They would be detected only if a Wittaia group had chosen the same hour and place to stage its own raid, or if the enemy had a magical defense post such as the one constructed near the banks of the same river by the Willihiman-Wallalua. This defense post was a small shelter about two and a half feet high, built on the plan of a common garden shelter and manned by alert ghosts, much as a watchtower is manned by alert men. When the ghosts saw an enemy patrol coming along the river bed, they leaped into the trees and shook them as a signal to warriors along the frontier.

Wereklué's party successfully avoided detection all morning as they worked their way toward the Wittaia gardens. While they moved forward, many men from all parts of the alliance, even as far as the brine pool, began to collect in Homoak, on the Anelerak, and by the *husuk,* the underground source of the Aikhé where it springs out from the eastern valley wall. These places are too far from the nearest Wittaia watchtowers to be seen. Later the uncommonly large numbers of armed men began to move in an almost endless stream up the near bank of the

Aikhé toward the Wittaia. They had to judge their departure so as to bring them within fighting distance in time to be of assistance to the raiding group. By two o'clock in the afternoon the supporting groups were in place and waiting for a signal that would come from the enemy as well as their own comrades once the attack was launched.

Unknown to both the raiders and the supporting group was the fact that the party led by Tegé Warek had been seen by a watchful Wittaia sentry. They were spotted far enough away that the Wittaia had time to organize a clever strategy called *weem mugisik,* a counterambush. In effect, the Wittaia simply permitted the fourteen Willihiman-Wallalua to penetrate their frontier and thereby come between two groups of hidden defenders. At the proper moment the trap was sprung, and in the struggle that followed, three men were wounded. Siba was hit by an arrow in the thigh, Tekman Biok by a spear in the hip, and Yonokma by an arrow in the knee joint. Greatly outnumbered, all the Willihiman-Wallalua ran away except Yonokma, whose wounded knee had crippled him. In the moments that followed, thirteen Willihiman escaped and one lay many times dead as the spears of enemy warriors were plunged needlessly into his inert body.

The sound of battle brought the waiting Willihiman-Wallalua and Wittaia warriors from their hiding places, and soon the whole swampy ground south of the Watibara was filled with shouting and running men. The news of Yonokma's death quickly passed through the ranks of his comrades and within minutes had spread to his own village.

It began to rain, and the cold evening chilled the hearts of everyone. They stood in forlorn humiliation, staring across the green valley through which they had recently crept so confidently, and waited, hands and arms wrapped tightly about their necks, until the Wittaia decided to give up the remains of their young warrior. With them by now were three suffering women—Yonokma's mother and two sisters. (The only time women come near a battleground is when their men have killed an enemy or when one of their own warriors has been killed.)

Soon the Wittaia, protected by a shower of arrows, brought Yonokma forward. The Willihiman-Wallalua, in turn, sent a volley of arrows ahead of their own warriors who went out into no man's land to fetch the body safely home. Fearful that the descending night would compound the calamity of the day by giving cover to a swarm of vengeful ghosts, they quickly built a litter and carried him swiftly homeward. As the litter passed the Watibara, the silent watchers filed off the hill and joined the sad procession. The only sounds were those of feet sucking in the muck of the swampy trail and the sobbing dirge of Yonokma's forsaken women.

At twilight, when the procession reached Hellerabet, the central watchtower of the Willihiman-Wallalua defense, men plucked the bits of magic fern and grass that the Wittaia had inserted in Yonokma's wounds, rectum, and in a hole dug at the ventral base of his penis. To counter such ugly and menacing magic, the blood of a freshly killed pig was rubbed over the dead man's body. As a symbolic promise of revenge, and to certify the inescapable consequences in store for the Wittaia, Asuk, a kinsman of Yonokma, shot four grass arrows over the corpse in the direction of the enemy. Because of his distinction as a leader and his responsibility for the events of the day, Wereklué picked up another grass arrow and waved everyone home, taking time personally to comfort Iterhebilek, Yonokma's father, with his arm around the old man's cold shoulders. Then he turned, and like some ageless conductor striving to harmonize the terrible din of all human concerns, lifted the wand of his authority toward the enemy and cursed them.

Though it took a long time, because the Willihiman-Wallaluas' confidence in themselves was badly shaken over the loss, both Weaké and Yonokma were eventually avenged and the ghostly imbalance created by their deaths was finally righted. Soon both sides were preoccupied with obligations to those more recently killed, and the delicate scales governing life and death among the Dani continued to adjust to alternating fortunes. In a year, the toll on each side of deaths resulting from wounds received in formal battle, ambush or raids will number between ten and twenty. An equal or even greater number of Dani perish prematurely from complications arising from the common cold; hence, since Dani war is an institution involving virtually all male members of the society, the death rate is not excessive.

War is one of the paramount institutions of Dani life. With agriculture and pig raising, it constitutes one of the few major focuses of all people's interest and energy. Without it, the culture would be entirely different; indeed, perhaps it could not find sufficient meaning to survive except parasitically as the novelty of missionaries or policemen.

[144]

6 Violence

p. 151 : **281.** Groups of warriors, who are accustomed to fighting as a unit, cluster around the outermost watchtowers before advancing to the battle line. These groups are composed of friends and neighbors and have no formal organization.

pp. 152–153 : **282.** The war leaders talk to their warriors before going into battle. These leaders are respected men who can influence but not actually command their fellows. In battle, as in so many other activities, the Dani are gregarious individualists.

p. 154 : **283.** Behind the lines during a battle, the warriors are often content to simply watch the progress from a low hill. Except when they are on the actual front, the men at a battle are relaxed. As they watch the events at the front, they gossip, smoke cigarettes and meet friends from other areas who have come to participate.

p. 155 : **284.** An important war leader exhorts his warriors before the battle.

p. 155 : **285.** Waiting for their turn at the front, armed men shout toward the battlefield. Their shouts, although rarely heard or heeded, contribute to the confusion and excitement of the battle.

p. 156 : **286.** Warriors watch the battle from a rocky crest, safe for the moment even from stray arrows.

p. 157 : **287.** Warriors of a fighting unit run toward the battle with their weapons: long jabbing spears, short throwing spears and bows and arrows. The forces on a battlefield are evenly divided between spearmen and archers, but this is more the result of individual preference than of group strategy.

p. 158 : **288.** Young men watch a battle from a distance, learning by observation what they must know for the time when they will join in the battle itself. They will not be forced into battle, and some will never participate. Such youths may never become leaders of the first order, but they will not be made to suffer for their disinclination to fight.

p. 159 : **289.** At the front the two sides threaten each other, shouting and waving feather plumes. As they dart about they shoot arrows at likely targets. The smaller spears are sometimes thrown, but the carefully made banded spears, sometimes fifteen feet long, are mainly jabbing weapons. They are too valuable to be thrown except when the target is certain.

p. 159 : **290.** A young warrior, a leaf bandage covering a wound received earlier in the day, watches the battle.

p. 160 : **291.** A wounded man is carried from the front on the shoulders of a friend.

p. 160 : **292.** Men often suffer minor wounds from arrows. At the front a warrior can see and dodge most arrows, but when he withdraws, he is likely to be hit in his back or buttocks. Thus it is the bravest men, those who have been most active in battle, who are most likely to be wounded in the rear. Occasionally a man who has been standing inattentively behind the lines, thinking that he was beyond range of the enemy, is also hit by a stray arrow.

p. 160 : **293.** Near the front the two sides shout and gesture at each other.

p. 160 : **294.** A Dani surgeon uses a bone needle to remove a barbed arrow.

p. 161 : **295.** An arrow is removed from a man's leg. Anyone can try his luck at removing an arrow, but a few men are well known for their surgical skill and spend much of their time at a battle, operating on their unfortunate comrades.

p. 161 : **296.** Crouching warriors try to move unseen toward the front.

p. 161 : **297.** In the safety of the rear lines, a skilled surgeon attempts the delicate removal of a barbed arrow from a friend's leg. Unless extreme care is used, the tip of the arrow will break off in the wound and cause it to fester.

pp. 162–163 : **298.** A battle in progress.

p. 164 : **299.** A boy who is too young to fight watches and learns from the safety of a watchtower. Young boys often bring their play weapons to battle, but stay far to the rear, in the company of the older men, the wounded and those who are not inclined to fight that day. Women are never seen at a battle, although they often work in their gardens within hearing distance.

p. 164 : **300.** The front lines.

p. 164 : **301.** A boy advances with a throwing spear. This sort of spear, like the regular fighting or jabbing spears, is made of hardwood and can do considerable damage. But no attempt is made to straighten it, and it lacks the woven band which is always placed on a jabbing spear.

p. 164 : **302.** A war leader shouts directions which are often unheeded at the height of battle. Such a man has particular responsibility for the battle, and the course of the fighting is supposed to reflect his general influence with the ghosts.

p. 165 : **303.** During most of the day a battlefront remains stable. But sometimes one side will mount a sudden charge and the front will shift rapidly, stringing warriors out along a ridge.

p. 165 : **304.** Tension at the front.

p. 165 : **305, 306.** Two spearmen.

Battlefield Surgery

p. 166 : **307.** A wounded youth is rushed back from the battle.

p. 166 : **308.** The arrow tip is pulled from his chest.

p. 166 : **309.** When the arrow is removed, cuts are made in the belly skin to drain away the "dark blood."

p. 166 : **310.** The injured youth is sprinkled with refreshing water.

p. 166 : **311.** A moment of rest and perhaps shock.

p. 166 : **312.** The severely wounded are carried to their village, sometimes miles away.

p. 167 : **313.** The tip of the arrow has penetrated deeply.

p. 168 : **314.** Weyak in battle.

p. 168 : **315.** The exuberance of battle.

p. 168 : **316.** An army withdraws from battle.

p. 168 : **317.** The front.

p. 168 : **318.** A warrior.

p. 169 : **319.** The front line.

p. 170 : **320.** A warrior with an arrow in his chest.

p. 170 : **321.** Leaf bandages have been lashed to the arrow wound and the belly skin is sliced.

p. 170 : **322.** The three belly slits drain the "dark blood."

p. 170 : **323.** An older man blows strength back into the wounded man. The shock of the wound has driven the man's **etai-eken,** or soul matter, toward his backbone, and the blowing is supposed to soothe it and draw it forward again into its proper place.

p. 171 : **324, 325.** A small magical bundle is held to the wounded man's **etai-eken** to revive it.

p. 171 : **326.** The stretcher is made.

p. 171 : **327.** The wounded man waits as the stretcher takes shape.

p. 171 : **328.** Leaf bandages are lashed on.

p. 171 : **329.** The wounded man is laid on the stretcher.

p. 171 : **330.** The warrior is covered with grass to conceal him in his weakness from the ghosts.

p. 171 : **331.** He is carried home on a stretcher.

283

284

285

286

289

290

291

295

296

297

[161]

300

303

304

305

306

307

308

309

310

311

312

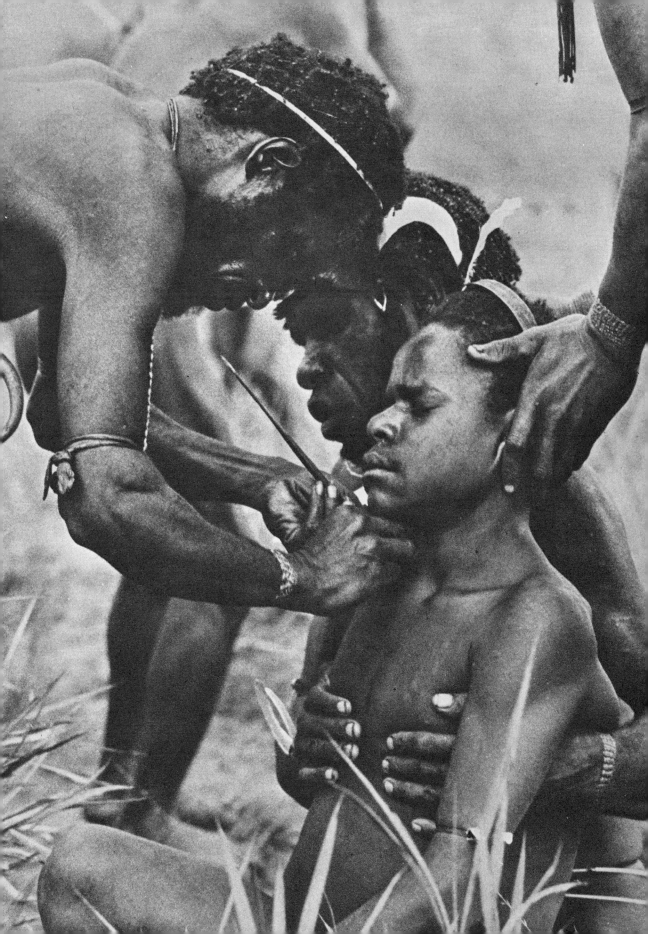

314

31

316

31

3

319

320   321   322

323

324

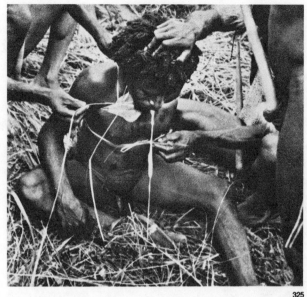

325

326

327

328

329

330

331

Photo Credits

The 337 photographs in this book were selected from a total of some 18,000 black and white photographs and 8,500 color photographs which were taken by the members of the Harvard-Peabody Expedition in the Baliem Valley between February, 1961, and December, 1963. The credits are indicated by the initial of the photographer:

(B) – Jan Th. Broekhuijse
(E) – Eliot Elisofon
(G) – Robert Gardner
(H) – Karl G. Heider
(M) – Peter Matthiessen
(P) – Samuel Putnam
(R) – Michael C. Rockefeller

COLOR SECTION
1 (R)   2 (H)

CHAPTER 1

3 (R)	7 (R)	11 (P)	15 (H)	18 (G)	21 (H)	24 (H)	27 (E)
4 (P)	8 (E)	12 (H)	16 (H)	19 (H)	22 (H)	25 (P)	28 (R)
5 (R)	9 (G)	13 (H)	17 (R)	20 (H)	23 (P)	26 (P)	29 (G)
6 (G)	10 (E)	14 (R)					

COLOR SECTION
30 (R)   31 (G)   32 (H)   33 (R)

CHAPTER 2

34 (H)	42 (H)	50 (H)	57 (H)	64 (H)	71 (E)	78 (E)	85 (B)
35 (H)	43 (B)	51 (G)	58 (H)	65 (H)	72 (H)	79 (E)	86 (B)
36 (H)	44 (H)	52 (H)	59 (H)	66 (H)	73 (H)	80 (G)	87 (E)
37 (R)	45 (E)	53 (E)	60 (H)	67 (H)	74 (H)	81 (H)	88 (R)
38 (B)	46 (H)	54 (H)	61 (H)	68 (H)	75 (H)	82 (B)	89 (H)
39 (H)	47 (H)	55 (H)	62 (R)	69 (H)	76 (H)	83 (B)	90 (H)
40 (H)	48 (H)	56 (H)	63 (H)	70 (M)	77 (H)	84 (B)	91 (H)
41 (H)	49 (R)						

CHAPTER 3

92 (R)	96 (H)	100 (H)	104 (R)	108 (H)	111 (E)	114 (H)	117 (H)
93 (R)	97 (R)	101 (P)	105 (H)	109 (H)	112 (H)	115 (R)	118 (H)
94 (H)	98 (P)	102 (E)	106 (P)	110 (H)	113 (P)	116 (H)	119 (R)
95 (R)	99 (H)	103 (E)	107 (H)				

COLOR SECTION

120 (H)	124 (H)	128 (R)	131 (P)	134 (H)	137 (H)	140 (E)	143 (R)
121 (H)	125 (P)	129 (H)	132 (P)	135 (R)	138 (H)	141 (P)	144 (R)
122 (R)	126 (H)	130 (G)	133 (H)	136 (H)	139 (G)	142 (R)	145 (R)
123 (H)	127 (P)						

CHAPTER 4

146 (R)	151 (H)	155 (H)	159 (R)	163 (R)	167 (G)	171 (R)	175 (E)
147 (H)	152 (H)	156 (H)	160 (R)	164 (R)	168 (H)	172 (H)	176 (E)
148 (H)	153 (H)	157 (R)	161 (R)	165 (P)	169 (R)	173 (R)	177 (R)
149 (H)	154 (R)	158 (R)	162 (R)	166 (R)	170 (H)	174 (H)	178 (G)
150 (H)							

CHAPTER 5

179 (B)	192 (H)	205 (H)	218 (G)	231 (R)	244 (R)	257 (H)	270 (P)
180 (H)	193 (M)	206 (H)	219 (G)	232 (R)	245 (B)	258 (R)	271 (P)
181 (G)	194 (H)	207 (R)	220 (B)	233 (R)	246 (R)	259 (R)	272 (P)
182 (H)	195 (E)	208 (H)	221 (B)	234 (H)	247 (R)	260 (B)	273 (E)
183 (B)	196 (H)	209 (R)	222 (R)	235 (R)	248 (R)	261 (P)	274 (R)
184 (M)	197 (H)	210 (M)	223 (R)	236 (G)	249 (R)	262 (E)	275 (R)
185 (B)	198 (H)	211 (H)	224 (B)	237 (G)	250 (R)	263 (E)	276 (R)
186 (H)	199 (H)	212 (B)	225 (M)	238 (G)	251 (H)	264 (P)	277 (R)
187 (H)	200 (H)	213 (H)	226 (R)	239 (G)	252 (H)	265 (P)	278 (P)
188 (H)	201 (H)	214 (R)	227 (R)	240 (G)	253 (B)	266 (R)	279 (E)
189 (R)	202 (H)	215 (B)	228 (R)	241 (R)	254 (B)	267 (R)	280 (R)
190 (R)	203 (B)	216 (R)	229 (R)	242 (R)	255 (M)	268 (R)	
191 (R)	204 (H)	217 (H)	230 (R)	243 (R)	256 (M)	269 (P)	

CHAPTER 6

281 (R)	288 (R)	295 (H)	302 (R)	309 (H)	316 (E)	322 (M)	328 (B)
282 (R)	289 (R)	296 (M)	303 (E)	310 (H)	317 (H)	323 (B)	329 (B)
283 (P)	290 (R)	297 (H)	304 (R)	311 (H)	318 (R)	324 (H)	330 (B)
284 (R)	291 (R)	298 (H)	305 (R)	312 (H)	319 (R)	325 (H)	331 (B)
285 (R)	292 (R)	299 (R)	306 (P)	313 (R)	320 (M)	326 (B)	332 (B)
286 (R)	293 (P)	300 (H)	307 (H)	314 (R)	321 (M)	327 (B)	333 (P)
287 (R)	294 (H)	301 (P)	308 (H)	315 (R)			

COLOR SECTION

334 (R)	335 (P)	336 (R)	337 (B)

Index

Page references for illustrations are in *italics*